THE Turtle PRIEST

A Transformation from HEAD TO HEART

Shane Wasinger (signature)

Shane Wasinger

outskirts press

Outskirts Press, Inc.
http://www.outskirtspress.com

Paperback ISBN: 978-1-9772-2134-6
Hardback ISBN: 978-1-9772-2118-6

Outskirts Press and the "OP" logo are trademarks belonging to Outskirts Press, Inc.

PRINTED IN THE UNITED STATES OF AMERICA

Dedicated to:

My father, Leonard R. Stoppel
who died too young
1943-1965

My uncle, Brother Emmanuel Wasinger, O.S.B. Cam.
monk of New Camaldoli Hermitage, Big Sur, CA
1927-2017

A close friend, Agnes A. Wind
who showed me the importance of gratitude
1922-2018

"The Turtle's teachings are so beautiful. So very special. It teaches us that everything you are, everything you need and everything you bring to the world is inside you, not external, and you carry it with you, and are not limited to a place, space or time."

— Eileen Anglin

Contents

PART 3: 2013–2019

Acknowledgments

I would like to thank a few people who indirectly or directly made this book possible to write.

First, I am thankful to Deacon Steve Maier and Deacon Ripperton Riordan for their assistance in arranging my time away for renewal and the opportunity to write this manuscript. Thank you Archbishop Bernard Hebda of the Archdiocese of Saint Paul and Minneapolis, Minnesota who granted my sabbatical leave.

To my parishioners of Saint Gregory the Great in North Branch and Sacred Heart Catholic Church in Rush City, Minnesota, thank you for your support and prayers while I was away for five and a half months.

I am most grateful for the seven-week sabbatical program which focused on personal renewal through prayer and reflection. This was offered by the Redemptorist Fathers at Saint Mary's Monastery, Kinnoull, Perth, Scotland in the Fall of 2018. I enjoyed my small sabbatical group who I shared this experience with and who also supported me during my preparation of writing this book. I couldn't come across a more valuable sabbatical course or group that genuinely brought new meaning to my ministry and life.

To the parishioners of Our Saviour's Catholic Church in Cocoa Beach, Florida and pastor Father Val De Vera, for welcoming me into their faith community and for their friendship, support and prayers while I wrote this manuscript.

A deep appreciation to Derek Harshman of Heathy Evolution

Fitness in Cocoa Beach, and his excellent mentoring and motivating skills while helping me in my physical training.

Thank you, my Aunt Sweetie Lamb and Uncle Terry Stoppel, for your part in my life without your brother and my father known to family and friends as Sonny.

I am honored to have my cousin Colin Lamb and nephew Tyler Betz as my godchildren and as well as being a Confirmation sponsor to Peter Leo, Jeffrey Lee, and Garrett Anderson.

Over the years, my cousins, the Saunders sisters, Tina Norman, Carrie Reedy, and Jennifer Craig, shared with me the stories of our growing up together. Thanks for all the good and not so good memories.

Thanks to Robert Rawson who has taught me so much about my faith by his actions and conversion and baptism into the Catholic faith.

Jackie Bleess' insights have proven to be instrumental in my personal and faith life. Thank you.

I am thankful for my Mother, Joan Wasinger, for the gift of life, your love, and passing on the Catholic faith and for sharing many memories, particularly in the early years of my existence.

To Dan and Diana Graff, I will be forever grateful for your friend-ship and generous hearts. Thank you for allowing me to live and write in your condo in Cocoa Beach overlooking the Atlantic Ocean while I wrote this book. It was the most inspirational spot I could ever have to write.

For reading this book in manuscript form, for your gracious comments, insights, and suggestions, thanks to Denny Adrian, Claire Kind, and Father Thomas Fitzgerald.

Deep gratitude to Kristen Radford and Douglas Werner for their editing skills which were invaluable.

To Kathy Altmanshofer and her keen eyes in reviewing, editing, and proofreading this book, not once but twice.

I am indebted to my cousin Sue Park who unbeknownst to her, planted the seed, many full moons ago, to inspire me to write this story.

Finally, to my dear friend Joan Hetherington, thank you for everything...to be accepted unconditionally by another human being is the greatest gift one can ever receive in this life.

Author's Note

In late spring of 1984, as the owner, my manager, and I looked out the window from the retail store we were in, we all saw a car collision occur at an intersection. When the police arrived, they asked each of us to give them a detailed description of what happened. To my surprise, each of us had a different narrative of the accident. How could that be? We all had seen the same accident.

In the book *Irresistible*,[1] the author writes about a group of seventh-graders learning about the American Revolution. The point he was making was that in their disagreement of what occurred, "they (seventh-graders) also learned that the truth is complex; that different parties may view the same event differently …" What was the truth?

In this book, I invite readers to see that the events of my life and the feelings which I have about those situations are my truth. One's feelings can only be the truth of that particular individual. Accordingly, I make no judgements or have any criticism of any of the persons in this book. In some cases, they may see an event or situation in a completely different viewpoint with their own feelings. Their feelings are the truth as my feelings are the truth.

---

1   Alter, Adam. 2017. *Irresistible: The Rise of Addictive Technology and the Business of Keeping Us Hooked*. Penguin Publishing Group: New York, p. 304.

PART 1
1962–1990

"In everything, whether it is a thing sensed or a thing known, Himself is hidden within"

— *Saint Bonaventure*

Prologue

A decision casually made by a driver in his early twenties to get behind the wheel of his vehicle in the early morning of November 1, 1965, forever altered the course of the lives of many families.

Approximately sixty miles earlier, this young man had been stopped outside Dodge City by the Kansas State Highway Patrol for driving erratically. Released to continue his journey, the drowsy driver made his way past Garden City and turned north on Highway 83. The road was a straight line, with the exception of a long curve located at the Finney-Scott county line, between Garden City and the next town of Scott City. He was now south of the boundary, amidst the oil-rich land of southwest Kansas where Century Refinery dominated the landscape.

Four men, all in their early twenties, completed their shift at the refinery at midnight, hopped into their car, and headed south to their homes in Garden City. Two of the passengers who sat on the right side of the car would never arrive home that night. Traveling south, only eleven miles from their destination, the tired driver who had fallen asleep at the wheel entered their path home. The driver crossed the white line and crashed head-on into the refinery workers' vehicle. In an instant, two of the men were killed. The front passenger was Leonard Stoppel—my father. The impact was so enormous his boots were forced off, and one was never found. Behind him sat Terry Brungardt, who was also killed in the crash.

One negligent man's decision on November 1, 1965, impacted the lives of many families, forever changing the course of many lives.

CHAPTER 1

The Funeral

It was Halloween, the day before the accident, and another typical, mild, cloudless day in southwestern Kansas. My mother stood in the kitchen preparing lunch for my father, who was getting ready to work the afternoon shift from 4:00 p.m. to midnight. When she finished making his sandwich, she placed it in his lunchbox. My father invited her to come and sit by him while he began playing his guitar. He enjoyed performing and loved singing for his wife.

As he stood up to leave, he kissed my mother—the woman he had wooed from across the street. He had married the love of his life four years earlier at Saint Mary's Church, which was located a few blocks east. Turning to his son and only child, he picked me up and began swinging my three-and-a-half-year-old body through the air, which instantly caused laughter and giggles. Putting me back on the ground, he gave both Mother and me a kiss followed by an "I love you." Mother repeated the words to him while I cutely uttered, "I luv you."

As my dad walked out of our home, he looked back with his boyish smile and said, "See you both tonight after work." These would be the last words ever spoken to his family.

Around 1:30 in the morning, the phone rang. It rang three times before my mom could awaken herself enough to answer it. On the other end of the line, she recognized the caller immediately—it was my grandfather, Ernie Stoppel. The Kansas State patrol had contacted him.

Immediately her father-in-law informed her that "Sonny"—Dad's nickname—had been in a terrible accident on his way home from work.

"How serious is it?" asked Mom.

"We are supposed to go to the police station," replied Grandpa, continuing, "We will pick you up, and drop Shane at Sweetie's."

My Aunt Sweetie, whose actual name was Dolores, was my dad's older sister and lived nearby. After they dropped me off at my aunt's home, Grandpa, Grandma, and Mom drove to the police station. When they spoke to someone inside, they were told to go to a funeral home. After they reached the funeral home, they were advised to go to Saint Catherine's Hospital, a short distance away.

Upon entering the emergency entrance, a request came to my mom from one of the medical personnel to follow him. All three family members were ushered into the room where my dad's motionless body lay. The doctor removed the cloth covering him. Glass was driven into his dry, bloody face; Mom weakly stated, "Yes, it is him." At this point, she fainted and was carried outside the room and placed on a chair. We returned home, everything now blurred to my newly widowed mother.

When I woke up several hours later, Mom was sitting on a chair in our small apartment on Jenny Street. As Mom remained sitting, crying, I came to her, kneeled in front of her, placed my elbows on her knees, and with my hands holding up my cheeks looked up into her eyes and asked, "When is Daddy coming home?"

"He is not coming home," Mom announced sadly.

"Why?" I asked curiously.

"He has gone to Heaven," uttered Mom.

"Where is Heaven?" I questioned.

Using her right hand, she began pointing in different directions, revealing, "Heaven is over there, up there, under there—everywhere."

Since this revelation was too much for my three-and-a-half-year-old mind to grasp, I just looked up at Mom and simply, silently smiled as my mother continued to weep.

It was the third evening following Dad's tragic death. The Roman Catholic Church's tradition at the time was to have three funeral rituals, the first being a wake and Rosary service, which was held at one of the local funeral homes. My mother and my grandparents arrived early to view my father's body, dressed in a suit, in the coffin. Soon after, family and friends arrived offering their condolences and prayers.

When the time arrived to recite the Rosary, which was led by one of the priests from Saint Mary's Parish, my uncle Jerry carried me into the room and walked up close to the casket. My mom, Grandpa and Grandma Stoppel, and Grandma Irene Gunkel stood nearby, all of us looking at my dad.

Still held by my uncle I bellowed out, "Daddy is sleeping!" At that moment, my mom and other close family members began to sob with grieving hearts for their sudden loss of a husband, son, brother, and friend.

The following day, the second traditional Roman Catholic Church funeral rite, or celebration of the Holy Eucharist (known also as the Mass), took place at Saint Mary's Catholic Church; it was where Dad had also been baptized and received both of the sacraments of Holy Communion and Confirmation. The service lasted for about an hour, after which a procession of cars proceeded to Valley View Cemetery, situated on a hill on the northern edge of Garden City.

As soon as the funeral attendees assembled around the open

grave and coffin, a Catholic priest led the burial prayers—the final part of a Catholic funeral ceremony. After completing the prayers, military honors were performed since my dad had served in the US Army from 1961 to 1964. The service ended with the presentation of the American flag to my mother, his one true love, who will forever mourn what could have been.

CHAPTER 2

Farm Life

A few months after the death of my father, Mom and I moved to Aurora, Colorado, with my Uncle Jud and Aunt Sis. Joining us for a period of time were Tina and her younger sister Carrie, daughters of my mom's younger sister Arlene and her husband Gary. A year and a half later, Arlene gave birth to another daughter, Jennifer. These three sisters became my closest cousins since we would be together each summer for a few weeks either on the farm or in Idaho Springs, Colorado, where they lived.

Our stay in Aurora lasted until the middle of 1966. My mom received some insurance money from the accident during this time, and she purchased a trailer home which brought us closer to family in Hays, Kansas. Hays was the center of a Volga Russian-German community, home of my ancestors. Uncle Jud and Aunt Sis followed us once again and rented a home nearby.

Shortly afterwards, my dad's uncle Albert introduced a widower, Leonard Wasinger, to my mother. Len lived on a farm in Scott County, Kansas, a mile north of the Century Refinery where the north winds brought odors of processing oil into gasoline.

Leonard, who was much older than my mom, also lost his wife, Norma, in 1965. Like my father, Norma had also been killed in a car accident. Similarly, the accident occurred on US Highway 83; the distance between the two crashes on the same highway was only thirteen miles apart.

The fatal accident left Mr. Wasinger to raise a daughter, Kyra, and a son Kurt. Both his children were older than me at the ages of ten and five respectively. All the farm work barely allowed enough time for Len to take care of his two children, who had been sent to stay with his sister and family in El Paso, Texas.

Len was searching for a wife who could take care of his children while providing companionship. After a year of courtship, Len proposed to Mom. She accepted. On August 1, 1967, they were married at Saint Joseph's Catholic Church in Hays. Soon afterwards, we moved to his large corn and wheat farm in Scott County. This move turned out to be my second life-changing event.

My new dad legally adopted me and changed my surname from Stoppel to Wasinger. This name switch deeply hurt my birth father's family. I would not understand the extent of this decision until many decades later. To this day, I think of my new dad as my second dad[2] and my birth dad as my "real" dad. Ironically both dads were named "Leonard."

The following May, my mom, who was in labor, instructed me to run out to the cornfield and fetch my dad. Immediately my parents drove to Saint Catherine's Hospital in Garden City, where Mom gave birth to a healthy baby girl—my sister Lori.

Roughly fifteen months later, Mom gave birth to her third and final child. Born on my parents' second wedding anniversary, August 1, Christopher Paul entered the world. He had suffered a lack of oxygen during his delivery, which created a lifetime of medical problems. The complications from his birth were not diagnosed until six months later when he was admitted to Children's Hospital in Denver. This began a series of long stays in medical centers in Denver as well as Broad Street Hospital in Philadelphia, which was

---

2   Throughout the rest of this book, when writing "dad," it refers to Leonard Wasinger. When referring to Leonard Stoppel, I will write "my birth dad."

known at the time for its expertise in neurological medicine. My brother's mishandled delivery by the attending physician became the third momentous life-changing episode in less than four years.

The next six years living on the farm proved to be both a blessing and a curse. It was a magnificent, safe environment in which to grow up while at the same time was an atmosphere of isolation and innocence regarding life realities. Chris' health required more and more of my mom and dad's time, and even with the support of volunteers aiding in his care, I received less time and attention. Mom and Dad would take turns, several weeks at a time, staying with Christopher in the hospital. Living with his disability kept me on an emotional roller coaster. More than once, I was informed that Christopher was dying and to prepare to say good-bye. Each time, he would pull through. I loved my brother; however, reflecting back I often resented the time and energy Christopher's illness required from my family, as it left me feeling ignored and insignificant as a child. Mostly, I wasn't taught the importance of sharing my feelings as my family didn't discuss their feelings. I'm certain this led to my inability to develop relationships with others. Our German ancestry with one of its characteristics of keeping one's feelings to oneself, along with my dad's alcoholism, would also thwart my ability to function relationally as a healthy adult for the majority of my life.

My stepbrother, Kurt, and I (22 months apart) shared a bedroom and played together as naturally as two blood brothers. Every day we rode school bus #17 to and from Shallow Water Grade School, three miles north of our farm. Outside of school while on the farm, he was my best friend. Building forts out in the cornfield was one of our favorite pastimes. In the mid- to late summer when the corn stood tall, we made a path through the cornfield about forty feet long. We cleared another 8 by 8 feet and attached chopped cornstalks to the nearby remaining stalks to construct a roof. During harvesttime, Dad would discover all of our forts, which for some reason didn't sit well with him.

One summer day, while Mom and Dad were in town, Kurt and I decided to burn the trash inside some old barrels located some distance from our house. We found matches inside the house, which we knew very well were off-limits for us. We laughed as we watched the flames grow and smoke bellow from the barrels. The following day, my mom was taking out the trash when she observed the charred trash barrel.

When she found us, she asked us if we burned the trash. Kurt didn't say a word, but I told the truth. This caused displeasure for my brother since then we would be in trouble. As our punishment, we both had to write on the chalkboard one hundred times, "I will not play with matches." Lesson learned.

Since that day, Mom considered me to be a truthful and honest child. "You are so honest, Shane," Mom would often say. As the years went by, however, I wasn't always as truthful as she thought, whether it was through repeated white lies, by simple omissions, or unkept promises. Once when my parents went to town for several hours, my brother Kurt and I attempted our cooking skills. Mom had specially told us, "Don't use the oven!" Upon their return, the smell of burnt cookies still wafted through the air. There was no denying that we had directly disobeyed her orders. We hadn't kept our promise. This flaw in my character became grander as the years passed.

From kindergarten through sixth grade, I attended Shallow Water Grade School. Besides Kurt and I, seven other Wasinger children attended the school—the children of two of Dad's brothers' families, who lived a short distance on nearby farms.

The comfort, assertiveness, and security I experienced at school allowed me to experience some socialization as I participated and organized class projects from time to time. For one project, students wrote letters to other students, sharing a little about themselves, and then asked for the other student to write back to us, telling us about themselves. This began my love for writing letters, and I would continue to carry on this passion by reaching out to others through cards and notes (doing my best to support the US Postal Service) throughout my lifetime. The self-confident and outgoing nature I felt during my elementary years began to gradually wither away when our family moved to Garden City, Kansas, in August 1974.

CHAPTER 3

Teenage Years

Anticipation filled the air as our six pickup caravan drove twenty-five miles south to Garden City and our new home on Fitz Street. This relatively new housing development on the east side of town would prove to be quite the change for me. The move wasn't the only change I encountered. In August, my half-brother Kurt was sent to Saint Thomas More prep school in Hays. At this time, I began attending Abe Hubert Junior High School, where I either walked the mile to and from school or found a ride with a next-door neighbor whose only son was a year ahead of me.

Enormous in population, my new school had three hundred in each grade from seventh to ninth. Needless to say, adapting from one teacher and a classroom size of eleven, to being taught by different instructors for the six periods of the school day and with different classmates, created a challenge which was difficult for me to overcome. Very few friendships were created. Moreover, other than my involvement in the school's Science Club, the only other activities I participated in at this time were one block away at Saint Dominic Catholic Church, where I served as an altar server. I also had a job as a newspaper delivery boy for the *Garden City Telegram* as well as selling the *Grit*, a former weekly newspaper, door to door.

Our family continued to embrace the Roman Catholic faith from top to bottom. Both my First Communion and First Confession had taken place at Saint Joseph's Church in Scott City, where we devotedly attended Sunday Mass—never missing a single Sunday service! Once when camping in the Colorado Rocky Mountains, against Mom and our wishes, my dad made us get up and go to the local parish for Sunday Eucharist. In addition to weekly Mass, we attended faith formation classes almost every Saturday during the school year. Mom even taught one class at that time; later she would become the faith formation coordinator at Saint Dominic Parish Community.

We lived in a traditional Catholic home, not only supporting our priests by inviting them over for dinner, but also financially by giving the parish substantial donations. The encouragement we gave to our priests went beyond meals and monetary gifts. They were also involved in our lives. For instance, Monsignor Heisman and Father Hiem, who served in our parish and at Saint Catherine's Hospital while we lived on Fitz Street, took a week-long fishing vacation to Mexico with Dad, Kurt, and myself. We flew to Mexico in a small private airplane and had a great time fishing and soaking up the warm sun! Growing up, I felt it was normal to attend Mass regularly. That was what my family did. Having priests for family friends only strengthened my faith formation and wanting to become a priest felt as natural to me as getting married felt to others.

On another occasion, the happy, friendly, and holy Monsignor once took several of us boys from our local parish to Sacred Heart Cathedral in Dodge City to watch a priesthood ordination. There were religious vocations within my own family: a great aunt was a sister in a Wichita convent and my dad's brother, Emmanuel, was a Camaldolese brother, or monk, in Big Sur, California. It was not surprising another would emerge from within our family.

The first notion of a possible priestly vocation started back on the farm, and continued to develop, while residing on Fitz Street, until I was twelve to thirteen years old. As on the farm, I would dress up and play a priest. My sister Lori and brother Chris, along with my cousins Tina, Carrie, and Jennifer, whenever they would come to visit, our family dog, and a wide assortment of dolls and stuffed animals, served as my congregation.

Acting as a stern priest, I often hollered at my "congregation" to be quiet and behave, which they purposefully would not. Chris added to the problem, since my yelling encouraged him to giggle, and when my sister or cousins would ask him to be quiet, which he really couldn't understand, he would laugh all the more.

When the time arrived for "Communion," I gave them soggy crackers and Kool-Aid pretending they were the Body and Blood of Christ. We did this repetitively; however, after playing Mass several times in a row, one of my "followers" would usually inform me they were bored, and my congregation immediately dispersed. To this day, whenever we see each other, we share stories with smiles and laughter as we recall our mock Sunday Masses at home.

I began to entertain a priestly vocation with a desire to attend a minor seminary for students aged fourteen through eighteen. My attraction to the priesthood led me first to look at a Franciscan seminary in Cincinnati, Ohio. My mom was terrified to see her thirteen-year-old son board an Amtrak train alone. However, she eventually allowed me to do so. The conductor on the train assured my mother he would look after me and make certain that my transfer to another train would go smoothly, which he did.

Upon my return from Cincinnati, I informed my parents that Saint Francis Seminary would suit me perfectly. They, on the other hand, shared a different opinion. My parents wanted me to think about entering Precious Blood Seminary, much closer to home, located in Liberty, Missouri, a suburb of Kansas City. I quarreled with them fruitlessly but ended up enrolling as a freshman in high school in the fall of 1976.

Precious Blood Seminary was administered by the Precious Blood Fathers and Brothers, a Catholic religious order founded by Saint Gaspar del Bufalo in Italy whose chrism is to proclaim the message of, "Believe in the power of the blood of Jesus, shed for all, to heal a broken world." They staffed Saint Mary's Parish in Garden City, where I had been baptized. Over the years, my family was accustomed to their preaching and service in the Catholic Church; logically it did make more sense to join their seminary than the one in Ohio.

I enjoyed my time at Precious Blood Seminary. The class size was similar to when I was at Shallow Water Grade School and offered me a chance to be away from home for the first time alone and gave me numerous quiet hours to pray in the chapel. My favorite class that year was English, taught by a newly ordained priest. The lessons learned and my enjoyment of the class remain with me to this day. I worked so hard in studying Spanish, as I always wanted to fluently speak a second language. Even with Father Joe's added support, I never managed to receive higher than a "D" each semester. This was due to my inability to clearly transcribe my thoughts through my words. Struggling with enunciating my words clearly, along with the inability to choose the correct words at times, was a disability I would live with throughout my lifetime. The hardest part was I knew that others did not understand me, which led me to bury the embarrassment of my inability to communicate clearly deep within me.

At the end of the school year, I sought to continue my priestly vocation into the next grade at the seminary; however, the formation team informed me they did not believe I was able to relate in a mature manner or was future priest material. I was hurt. Not priest material? What was I if I wasn't good enough to be a priest? This dismissal rendered the question of who I was and why couldn't I seem to fit in anywhere. Surely, I was faithful and compassionate like the priests I knew, yet what I considered good enough, once again, was not good enough for the rest of the outside world. Disheartened, I came back to my hometown where I finished out my high school years at Garden City Senior High School.

CHAPTER 4

Surviving Senior High School

Upon returning home from the seminary, I moved into another home which my family built. This was a two-story home with a finished basement and three-car garage located a few blocks west on Center Street. It was the end of May 1977, and the house provided a safe haven and place of comfort for me, especially since I was still saddened by having to leave the seminary. Kurt, now a senior in high school, and I were once again under the same roof, each of us occupying our own basement bedroom. Since he'd received his driver's license and own car, he drove us on most days to and from school.

At the end of the school year, against our dad's wishes, Kurt planned to get married. His soon-to-be wife was expecting his child. My father and Kurt argued but to no avail; Kurt married. Dad was upset and embarrassed by my brother, so he didn't allow any of our immediate family to attend the wedding. This resulted in a permanent estrangement between Kurt and my dad, and they no longer communicated from that point forward. Nevertheless, I visited Kurt, his wife, and child from time to time without my dad knowing. However, over the years Kurt and I eventually lost contact. I couldn't share my feelings with my dad about this decision, since he never listened to my side of things. I just had to be quiet and accept that my brother was not welcome in our home. Kurt's departure from our family permanently saddened me. It still does today, more than 30 years later. He is missed!

The summer before my junior year in high school, Dad purchased a light blue Dodge Dart with the money I'd earned raising and selling my 4-H livestock. On my 16th birthday, this newfound freedom of driving allowed me to get my first job as a produce clerk at Dillon's, the local grocery store on Main Street.

I worked along with another student from my high school most days in the produce department. Besides being friends, we were comrades among the other employees, all of whom we knew from school and/or church. On weekends, we would often go to parties at the homes of some of our bosses who were a few years older than us high-schoolers. Since my parents were either traveling to be with my brother Christopher in a Philadelphia hospital or taking an extended vacation, a few of the parties took place at our new Center Street home. Alcohol and illegal drugs were always obtainable at these gatherings through older peers or from my dad's liquor cabinet.

When these parties were at my house, a large mess would usually ensue. I would attempt to clean up as much as possible before my Grandma Gunkel arrived, just before my parents were to return. Once, my grandma found a Frisbee that she believed contained some dried-up crumbling plant. That plant actually was marijuana that a coworker left behind. When she asked what it was, I acted as if I didn't know and she threw the weed away.

I have not used any illegal drugs, not even marijuana. The drug of my choice was alcohol. Not only would I drink at these parties but also privately in my bedroom. Drinking gave me a release from the emptiness I felt as well as the sadness I felt at Kurt being tossed aside. Was I next? How can you do this to your own family? I could not understand this, and drinking helped me cope. Sometimes I even resented that my parents were gone so much taking care of

Christopher and his many health issues, although I loved my brother dearly. Added to all this was the fact I had to leave the seminary, one of the few places I had been happy. All these things would create the perfect storm for my drinking habit. Although the amount and frequency was minimal, it wasn't too long before I had my first terrible encounter with alcohol. Right before my senior year, someone gave me a pint-size bottle of Southern Comfort, which I drank in its entirety. The following morning, I experienced my first hangover. I was not proud of that incident and never shared it with anyone else.

I worked at Dillon's nearly two years until one day in April I became very angry at the store manager, abruptly quit, and walked out. I can't recall the reason for my unexpected outburst of rage. It wasn't until years later that a therapist would help me find where this rage inside me had come from. My action at Dillon's would be the first of other problematic behaviors that would result in misery for me as I continued to isolate my feelings.

On the whole, my three years going to Garden City Senior High School were as ordinary for me as for any other teenager; there were classes I liked and other classes I disliked. Extracurricular activities were limited to joining the Science Club and attending Friday night football games when they were played at home or at our rival's, the Dodge City Red Demons.

My favorite subjects were social studies, history, and astronomy. I believe that my fascination with social studies resulted from the isolation and lack of diversity I experienced on the farm. This isolation compelled me to seek out information and learn about the rest of our world. The appeal of studying human society remains with me to this day, as does my curiosity of astronomy. My interest in stars, night skies, and the universe was further developed by a favorite science teacher, Mr. Sanders. Likewise, the first term paper I ever wrote was about Nicolaus Copernicus and the Scientific Revolution.

While numbers, dates, and appointment times are easy for me to remember, more advanced forms of mathematics, such as algebra and geometry, did not hold my interest as they were arduous to comprehend. During my sophomore year, I skipped my geometry class for two weeks until the teacher realized that I wasn't attending class and contacted my parents. Even though I went to that class the rest of the semester, I received my one and only "F" in school. My other grades were typically "C" or above, permitting me to graduate on May 18, 1980, the same day that Mount Saint Helens volcano erupted in the state of Washington.

During my high school days, my sister Kyra wed Larry Fief at Saint Dominic Church in June 1977, and Kurt and I were altar servers at Mass. Kyra and Larry knew each other for about ten years, meeting the first time after Mom married my second dad. Once their wedding nuptials took place, Larry became my brother-in-law—in addition to already being my uncle. This became a baffling fact that has continually puzzled those who hear about the arrangement for the first time—until explaining that Larry (a twin) is my mom's youngest brother and Kyra is the daughter of my second dad.

The traditional photo-op ensued before the ceremony with some family pictures shot at our Center Street home, which was only two blocks away from the church. This particular day became one of the loveliest and most important memories for my mom's family. For the first time in their lives, all twelve siblings, seven boys and eight girls, were together under the same rooftop.

Eighteen months after the wedding, my Grandpa Stoppel died. Both Grandpa Fief, my mom's father, and Grandpa Wasinger died earlier in this decade. My grandpa passed away from cancer caused by his poor health due to his drinking and smoking. This information was not shared with me until forty years later when my Aunt Sweetie shared it with me.

Once again, my desire to become a priest reawakened during the latter part of my high school career. Through the encouragement of our parish priest, I contacted our diocesan vocation director at the offices of the Diocese of Dodge City. Soon after, I had an appointment to meet with our Bishop in the fall of 1979.

The young Most Reverend Eugene Gerber, who had only been a bishop for a few years, made a special visit to our home to discern my potential priesthood vocation and to consider the possibility of placing me as an incoming freshman at a college seminary in the fall. Without providing the location, Bishop Gerber gave me a list of three diverse college seminaries, sharing about each of their unique characteristics. After sharing this with me, he asked which one most appealed to me. It didn't take long for me to convey my answer.

Upon giving my response, the Bishop responded, "Good, I will arrange for you to go see and tour Conception Seminary College in northwestern Missouri."

"Thank you," I replied.

CHAPTER 5

~~

A Second Chance at Seminary

Two months after visiting with Bishop Gerber, I drove alone to northwest Missouri to tour Conception Seminary College near the town of Conception Junction. Overseeing the seminary were the monks from the Swiss-American Benedictine Abbey of Conception. In the center of Conception Abbey and Seminary stands the magnificent and spiraling Basilica of the Immaculate Conception, which was completed in 1891. The church, monastic, and seminary buildings are visible from a great distance when driving through the rolling hills of Nodaway County.

After exploring Conception, meeting many students, monks, and college staff (as well as a shirttail relative, Brother Michael), I felt at home. It didn't take me long to inform Bishop Gerber I wished to attend. After successfully completing the process to become a seminarian for the Diocese of Dodge City, I applied to Conception Seminary. I was accepted and began my studies in the fall of 1980.

At the start of the school year, we had around twenty-four in our class. Our individual rooms and communal bathrooms encompassed the top two stories of Saint Michael's Hall and our classes were held in the lower two floors. The rooms were simple, having old-fashioned water radiators and no air conditioning. My room faced the east, providing me scenic views of pastures, fields, and a pear tree orchard. The monks grew the tastiest pears that I have ever eaten to this day!

Our classes were held in Saint Michael's Hall and in the building immediately south, Saint Maur's Hall. Saint Maur's also housed the seminary administrative and staff offices, a recreational room, and a small bookstore. The chapel was located on the third floor, where we gathered for morning and evening prayers and daily Mass.

Throughout my freshman year, I enjoyed several classes. Our English professor introduced us to numerous authors, including what would become one of my favorite Catholic authors, Flannery O'Connor. Fr. Lawrence taught philosophy. The first time in college that I stayed up all night studying for an exam was for his class "An Introduction to Western Philosophy." My favorite class that year was Brother Thomas' "Western Civilization." His enthusiasm, humor, and passion for the subject, predominantly French history, produced in me an immense desire to continue learning about history throughout my life.

Just as at Precious Blood Seminary, I struggled miserably at another foreign language: Latin. Both semesters I received a "D" in the class. Mercifully, to become a priest by that time, one didn't have to absolutely grasp Latin. Had this been a prerequisite, I would have never been allowed to continue my seminary studies or be ordained a priest.

Each class had its own formation advisor (priest or brother) who lived on the same floor as his students. Each seminarian took part in spiritual direction, and we were allowed to choose our own spiritual director from a list that had been passed out at the beginning of the school year. Partway through the year I decided to switch directors, which went on to be an effective choice. After finishing the first year at Conception Seminary College successfully, I was happily invited to resume my studies the following fall.

I was not eager to return home during the summer months, so arrangements were made for me to spend this time with a host family in Hays. A middle-aged couple with their high-school-aged son offered me a small room in their rural home upon the request of their parish priest.

Despite the fact I had left my employment at the Garden City Dillon's store under poor circumstances, I was hired at the Hays store location. This grocery store was much larger, and once again I found myself in the produce department. My supervisor was laid-back, and my coworkers were easygoing and pleasant to work with.

Just when I was offered two weeks of full-time employment, I informed my produce manager that I was leaving Hays. Earlier in the day, my host mom notified me I needed to leave as she felt our living arrangement was not a good fit. No explanation was provided; I was shocked. It had been difficult for me to form a bond with them. I was an introvert, my thoughts hidden deep within me. Sharing my thoughts and feelings with others was a painful and fearful thing for me to do. When I did share and speak, the words I chose often did not make sense to others. I could never fathom why! How could I express that I know what is in my head, but I just can't get it across correctly! Once again, this episode caused me to feel I was not good enough and a failure at communicating with others.

Returning to my home, the summer passed by quickly, and soon I found myself traveling back to Conception Seminary on a hot and humid August day.

Three classmates had dropped out of the seminary over the summer, which left us with twenty-three in my sophomore year, as we also added two students. We lived on the top floor of Saint Joseph Hall, which had communal bathrooms, showers, and smaller rooms. My window faced the basilica, which was connected to the hall. The dining room dominated the bottom floor, while the abbey and seminary library occupied the middle space of the building. Our classes continued to be held in either Saint Maur or Saint Michael Halls.

Father Alexis served as our formation director during this second year. I resumed my spiritual director sessions with Father Martin from my previous year. He equipped me with aptitudes for a lifetime of spiritual discernment and introduced me to eminent spiritual gurus such as Thomas Merton, the famous Trappist of Gethsemani in Kentucky.

In the midst of my second year, I was assigned, along with three other seminarians, to do apostolic work at a group home for mentally and physically challenged men in nearby Albany. The Apostolic program required us to spend two hours almost every Saturday afternoon doing Christian service for others. At the group home, we interacted with the men in a variety of ways. This triggered more rage inside me. I disliked working at a community service activity that was so similar to that of growing up with Christopher. My memories of being told on countless occasions or offering myself to take Christopher to wash his hands and face kept running through my mind. I think to this day I enjoy sleeping in on Saturdays due to the fact that Christopher would wake up so early, and I was taking care of him before other family members rose in the morning. I knew it had to be done, but it reminded me so much of spending my life caring for my own brother and disliking how my childhood was changed because of this. I love my brother and would do anything for him, but this assignment kept reminding me of my past home life.

When the school year ended, I packed most of my belongings and stowed them in the attic of Saint Joseph Hall since I expected to return in the fall. Two days before our summer break, Father Alexis summoned me to come to his office stating he had something important to tell me.

Seated across the room of my formation advisor, he informed me that the formation team, comprised of four class formation directors, had made a decision about my future at the seminary. They concluded that I needed to "go experience the real world and have more and deeper relationships," and recommended I leave the seminary for a while to experience the outside world. I could return, Father Alexis said, but they suggested I complete my college studies outside the seminary and work on becoming a healthy individual. My thoughts were spinning as I attempted to comprehend what he just told me. My sheltered lifestyle had led me out into the world to experience more. I was content here!

Leaving his office, downtrodden, I went to see my spiritual director to discuss the affair. Father Martin and I spoke at length, and he concluded our talk with the advice to simply follow my heart. After exiting his office, I called Bishop Gerber. In our discussion, he felt that I should return to the seminary in the fall since I had merely been counseled to withdraw from the seminary but did have the choice of coming back.

Trusting in the formation team, listening to Father Martin, and pondering my Bishop's words, I chose to leave Conception Seminary College.

CHAPTER 6

On My Own

Saying good-bye to my life at Conception, knowing that I would not be coming back until two days before the summer break ended, I had no inkling where to go or what to do. Packing my belongings into the car, I headed west to Garden City, for a temporary stopover at our Center Street home. I didn't unload my vehicle. Then a few days later, once I visited my great-uncle Bill at Valley View Cemetery, where he worked as a caretaker, and told him what had recently transpired in my life and that I was going further west, I requested some money, which he obliged.

My travels took me to Greeley, Colorado, and then a small distance north to Ault, Colorado, where one of my seminary classmates' parents resided. Given a home-cooked meal and a comfortable bed, the following morning I left with the intention of continuing to head north and west to Wyoming. Another classmate lived in Kemmerer in the southwestern corner of the Cowboy State. Using a pay phone when getting closer to Kemmerer, I talked with a fellow student requesting a favor, which was to ask his pastor at Saint Columba's Catholic Church if he would permit me to lodge at the rectory while I decided what to do with my life. Appreciatively, he agreed. My stay would last a week. Prior to leaving Kemmerer, a stop was made at a liquor store where I bought my first bottle of alcohol, since the legal drinking age at the time in Wyoming was nineteen.

With a tentative plan in mind, and no specific reasoning, Fort

Collins, Colorado, became my destination. Arriving late in the afternoon, I was able to check into a hotel and begin my search for an apartment. My pursuit to locate a roof over my head was fruitful on the first day of hunting. An elderly couple was renting a basement apartment, and as soon as I saw it, I instantaneously fell in love with it.

My basement residence, with its private entrance, was inviting and cozy; a mural of the Rocky Mountains covered the west wall of the living room. Small in dimensions, the dwelling was well-matched to my living space needs. A complete kitchen and a small desk in the living room beside the bed was all I required. This first home in which I lived on my own continues to this day to be my favorite—the most Spartan one of all.

Soon I settled into my apartment and began to work on my next task, which was to obtain employment. Once again utilizing my connection with the Catholic Church, I contacted the nearby pastor of Saint Joseph's Church requesting a meeting with him. Father Nathan agreed to meet me the following day.

With his golden retriever named Oliver lying in front of his desk, Father Nathan inquired about my past and what line of work I previously had. I stated all of my employment had been in a grocery store as a produce clerk.

"Good," he declared, continuing, "there is a parishioner who is the manager of Toddy's Grocery Store. I will chat with him and see if an opening is available for you to fill."

Within a week, I started at Toddy's in the produce department. My manager was a cool guy and involved in his nondenominational Christian church. Our department employed several individuals from high school and college students to those in their early thirties. I became friends with a few coworkers, in particular one individual named Andy. He was from Oregon and enrolled at Colorado State University (CSU) in the town. We had several of the same interests and spent lots of time together going on walks and discussing our hopes and dreams in life. I believe Andy was the first true, best friend I'd had up to that point.

In order to receive in-state tuition, I worked for a year at Toddy's; even though I was not hired full-time, I found myself habitually working practically forty hours a week. In addition to working, other hours of the day were filled with my involvement at church, hanging out with my friends from work, and exploring Eastern philosophies and spiritualities.

At Saint Joseph, the pastor put me in charge of the altar servers, and I also volunteered as a part of the catechist team, teaching second-graders with another teacher named Jean. This was another friendship that would blossom during my stay in Fort Collins.

Father Nathan also encouraged me to share a meal with him and his associate at the rectory. Since he employed a cook, I took him up on his offer from time to time. We would meet once in a while, talking about numerous things. He once said that I would be a good writer, an encouragement that has stayed with me to this day—a reason for my seeking to be an author.

One day, a fellow coworker from Montana challenged Andy and me to join him on a three-day fast. Up to the challenge, I agreed. By agreeing to take part, not only did I feel excited, as it would be a new experience, but also, I was thrilled to be part of a group, giving me a sense of acceptance. We were victorious in our quest. I have continuously remembered the end of that three-day fast, the feelings of gratification and satisfaction derived from the experience, one that has never been duplicated, although attempted a few additional times.

I wasn't twenty-one and couldn't purchase or consume any liquor in Colorado, so just about every month, I would drive forty-seven miles north to Cheyenne, Wyoming. First, I stopped at a liquor store to buy a small bottle of Tanqueray Gin that would last me for a month. Then I continued with each visit to a restaurant within the Holiday Inn Hotel and ordered a mouthwatering French dip sandwich with fries and a single gin and tonic.

On the weekends when not going to Cheyenne, I would consume two or three drinks while watching the television. Other than going to the restaurant in Wyoming, I never drank anywhere else, including the bars. I never drank during the week, and my drinking neither increased nor decreased throughout my time spent living in Fort Collins.

Nine months after living in Fort Collins, I called home. Before chatting with Dad, I first spoke with Mom. With Dad, I talked about a car mechanical problem since he was knowledgeable in repairing cars, but something abruptly cut off our phone call. Neither one of us telephoned the other back. This would be the final time that I conversed with Dad.

Two weeks later, on the morning of March 26, Mom notified me that Dad had died some hours earlier of what they thought was a heart attack. At the age of fifty-three, his alcoholism had seized the life out of him. Thinking back, I can remember him buying a case of scotch at a time. He would often conceal it out of plain sight. Hiding liquor became a habit I would carry out in my later years. Twice he was admitted to treatment with unsuccessful results. Once he had driven off the road, probably due to his intoxication but never confirmed, only to be returned back home with the excuse that he had fallen asleep at the wheel. Back in those days, drinking while driving wasn't taken as seriously as it is nowadays.

The succeeding day the funeral arrangements were completed. The following week, a funeral Mass at Saint Dominic Church was held, and was followed by the procession and burial at Scott County

Cemetery where he was laid next to his first wife. We returned to the church for a funeral luncheon. Kurt came to the funeral service and meal. This was the very last time all five of us children would be together in the same room.

After living in Colorado for a year, I registered at CSU in the fall of 1983 as a history major and philosophy minor. Of the four classes signed up for, only my General Psychology course had over one hundred students, which intimidated me. The other three classes, specifically History of the Renaissance Age and Introduction to Eastern Religions, were enjoyable, mostly since each of the professors conveyed a passion for their subject.

The professor of the Eastern Religion course was a former Catholic priest who once belonged to a Trappist monastery and left to get married. We met a few times for dinner, talking about both his past and mine. I remember my Renaissance History instructor for what he taught me about writing a term paper. One of my essays was about Saint Charles Borromeo, a Catholic bishop living in the sixteenth century serving as the Archbishop of Milan for twenty years. Like Saints Ignatius of Loyola and Philip Neri, he was a prominent figure of the Counter-Reformation. My teacher deducted my grade from an "A" to a "B" since I had improperly written "Saint Charles Borromeo" instead of "Charles Borromeo," as he hadn't been declared a saint until after his death. This really made me feel angry, as I didn't feel this drop in a grade was justifiable.

My time attending CSU turned out to be short lived—just one semester. Three weeks before the end of first semester, Toddy's store manager and my produce department supervisor called me into the office. They said they had no choice but to fire me because of an incident earlier that week. A female employee and I clashed over something that I no longer recall, and in the midst of our disagreement I pushed a cart toward her, which she reported to our manager. Although the jostle caused no injury, it was enough to get me terminated.

I pleaded to keep my job. The firing was firm—there would be no negotiating! Once again, uncertainty eclipsed my future. Without an income and with no desire to search for another job, three weeks later I moved back to Garden City.

CHAPTER 7

Wandering Years

During an unusual cold stretch of weather, I started the eight-hour journey from Fort Collins to Garden City on January 1, 1984. After driving for two and a half hours, I stopped in Cope, Colorado, to see my cousin Tina, her husband, and her one-year-old daughter. I finished the remainder of my trip after this pleasant and reinvigorating visit.

A few months previous to my trip, my mom and Lori relocated to a new home on Pioneer Road, the first house built in a new development on the northern edge of Garden City. The basement of this brick home contained a small finished room, one-half of its area, which became my "bedroom" for the ensuing year.

I secured a job as a Filter Queen vacuum salesman soon after arriving in Garden City. The owner and manager of the local company promised me an enormous income and a comfortable lifestyle. This assurance appeared to be genuine. Since my family was well known in the area, including previous farm neighbors in Scott County, my first sales were prodigious. Convinced that I could create a generous livelihood for myself, after six months I opened my own vacuum cleaner store thirty-five miles away in Scott City.

For two more months, my sales continued to be amazing. Then suddenly one week, followed by another week, then a month, my vacuum sales plummeted. Imagining a comeback was unlikely, I decided to close the store in December and return to my college studies. Unfortunately, I still owned several expensive Filter Queen vacuum cleaners, which at some point would need to be sold.

1985 began as the previous one with a move to a new city, Lawrence, home of the University of Kansas (KU). Since on-campus housing was unavailable, which was my first preference, I moved into an apartment some distance away, which required me to take a bus to all my classes. Once again, I chose to major in history. Regrettably, unlike my classes at CSU, I found all my history courses rather dull, and agonizingly endured them to the end of the semester.

On the bright side, adjacent to the KU campus was the Saint Lawrence Catholic Campus Center, which was staffed by the priests of the Archdiocese of Kansas City, Kansas. Father Vincent served as its pastor. During his tenure he developed a magnificent spiritual home for KU's Catholic college students and others as well. Father Vince was an expert in fundraising and had a genuine passion for his ministry. Today this is one of the preeminent Catholic campus centers in the United States.

I asked Father Vince to be my spiritual director and, gratefully, he agreed. During my time at KU, we would meet every two weeks to discuss spiritual matters, and he would always offer valuable guidance which focused on my longing to become a priest.

Three-fourths of the way through the semester, my bank account totaled less than $5.00. For almost two weeks, I existed on water, jelly, and the biscuits I made from a box of Bisquick, which I paid for with a handful of quarters, dimes, and pennies. This was the poorest time in my whole life.

By the end of the school year, lacking a steady income, penniless, and incapable of paying my apartment rent, I hunted for summer work. Just outside the student center was a bulletin board with employment opportunities.

One particular employment opening announcement caught my eye. This specific notice would change the course of my future. The location and type of work advertised for the summer months sounded exotic and captivated my curiosity. The position was for a packer at the Gunflint Lodge and Outfitters, along the Gunflint Trail in northern Minnesota, fifty miles from the nearest town of Grand Marais, inside the Boundary Waters Canoe Area (BWCA).

I contacted the lodge. The person I spoke with was pleasant, answered all my questions, and addressed my apprehensions. After answering all of their questions, I was offered the job.

The following week, four employees from the lodge met me at the Grand Marias Greyhound bus station. The drive up the Gunflint Trail was amazing and scenic with wildlife, and we spotted a moose amongst the beautiful outdoors. As we entered the road in front of the lodge and outfitters, I asked myself, "What have I gotten into, coming to this strange and unknown land?" However, I soon settled into my new surroundings and found myself enjoying the work as a packer at the outfitters. The summer went by swiftly. We worked closely, having breakfast together each day before beginning our day. At last, I was creating friendships as we became more like family.

In mid-August when all the students were going off to college, it became obvious that even with my summer employment and savings, returning to school was not an option. The manager at the lodge offered to keep me on for another month, so I chose to stay. This became a time for me to really experience the Minnesota wilderness. The quiet life up north was stress-free. As an introvert, I don't handle stress well. This time provided me with the tranquility I longed for. Listening to the sounds of nature, especially the calls of loons, was far more enjoyable than I ever imagined it would be.

At the end of September, I returned to Garden City.

CHAPTER 8

Becoming a College Graduate

For the third consecutive January, I found myself on the road settling into a new place, this time in the Minneapolis and St. Paul Metro Area. I didn't have any reason to move to the Gopher State other than the fact it had been my home the previous summer. I packed all my possessions into my black Ford Mustang, departed Garden City the first week of January, stopped in Kansas City for a night, then continued to the Twin Cities with no housing or employment plans in place.

As soon as I entered the Twin Cities, the initial phenomenon I observed was the weather. When leaving southwestern Kansas, the temperature was 58 degrees. When I arrived in Minnesota, I was met with 17 degrees below zero, and two feet of snow saturated the landscape. By the end of my first Minnesota winter, I wondered if I had made a foolish decision to move here.

My first days in Minnesota were spent seeking work while living in a hotel, but not for long. I responded to a *Minneapolis Star-Tribune* ad for an apartment in Saint Louis Park where two young ladies sought an immediate third roommate. They guided me around the three-bedroom apartment as we shared bits of our lives with each other. They invited me to move in; however, they wanted to be clear that the lease would be up in six months with their intention of not renewing it. Having no apprehension, I moved in the subsequent day.

Now that I'd settled into a residence, the next task at hand was to acquire a place of employment, which happened quickly. The manager at the Brooklyn Park Holiday Stationstore hired me as a day assistant manager with the expectation in six weeks of transferring me to the Osseo location as a night manager.

For the next six months, I commuted seventeen miles back and forth to work. Before the apartment lease expired, I found a basement apartment with only a large room and a small bathroom, rented by a thirtyish woman, for an affordable price. The landlord and I shared the kitchen space, which functioned extremely easily since we had reverse hours with our employments. The living arrangements succeeded superbly.

Finally, at the age of twenty-four, I had created some stability for myself. I possessed a pleasant situation, and the hours working at the Holiday Station Store were just as amiable. Despite the fact I had settled down, my heart continuously yearned for something more out of life. My longing to become a Catholic priest persisted as fervently as ever. Nonetheless, it would be another two and a half years before my finances would allow me to pursue this.

During these years, I attended Mass and participated in a young adult Bible study at Saint Vincent de Paul Church in Osseo. While our weekly gatherings lasted approximately three months, one of the participants, a newly married man, and I continued to meet. From time to time we saw each other over a meal, speaking primarily about our spiritual lives. As our friendship grew, we eventually traveled to the BWCA for a week-long canoe trip.

In addition to my involvement in the Bible study, I visited with our pastor a handful of times since I was contemplating the prospect of returning to the seminary after my college studies were completed. He encouraged me to submit an application to the Archdiocese of Saint Paul and Minneapolis, which I did, as I was moving on to college in November 1989.

For the first time since settling on my own, my move to Saint Cloud, Minnesota, to attend Saint Cloud State University (SCSU) was a conscious decision which seemed sensible. After registering as a student and living on campus at the university, I transferred from the Osseo Holiday Stationstore to the Monticello one—a half-hour drive from Saint Cloud.

I shared a dorm room with two other students for six months until the summer arrived. Then one of my roommates, Dean, and I rented an off-campus apartment along with a friend of his and a fellow peer of mine, who was, like me, a philosophy major. During the summer I had the space all to myself and continued working in Monticello. As an assistant manager, there were 10-hour shifts starting at five in the morning, or the overnight shift which began at eleven in the evening.

Alone in my residence, I was unable to fall asleep and started drinking. Consuming a moderate amount of alcohol was all I required to sleep. During the previous six years, I drank insignificantly. Since alcohol only temporarily allowed me to sleep, I drank more and more to get the same outcome. Since I wasn't drinking heavily, or every day, my pattern went uninterrupted throughout the next year and a half. Given that drinking was part of college life, no one ever questioned my drinking habits.

When I began the application process to resume my seminary studies a year into my college career, an early caution was presented to me by a psychologist who was evaluating my maturity and mental health. As an integral practice in 1990 as today, the vocation director of the Archdiocese of Saint Paul and Minneapolis sought the recommendation of an outside psychologist's evaluation as to the maturity and emotional wholeness of all prospective seminarians. The psychologist concluded I was mentally apt to pursue my priesthood studies provided that I stay vigilant about any addictions. He indicated that my evaluation uncovered a trait in me that could possibly lead to addiction problems in the future. He further probed into my drinking habits and asked me how often I consumed alcohol. I lied, responding only once or twice a week. However, by that time, my drinking was now twice as much.

Receiving an affirmative endorsement from the psychologist and meeting all the requirements of the vocation office, I was admitted as a seminarian to the Archdiocese of Saint Paul and Minneapolis along with one stipulation: I would start off in the fall of 1990 as a pre-theology student instead of a first-year theology student at the Saint Paul Seminary School of Divinity of the University of Saint Thomas. Although disappointed, I moved forward. A few months later after graduating successfully with a bachelor's degree in philosophy, the vice-rectory of Saint Paul Seminary (SPS) notified me that my status was changed. Not only had I achieved the requirement for a philosophy degree, given my entrenched Catholic religious upbringing, I qualified to enter SPS as a first-year seminarian. I would recommence my priesthood formation, for the third time, in the fall of 1990.

PART 2
1990–2013

"Even in the life of a Christian, faith rises and falls
Like the tides of an invisible sea. It's there,
Even when he can't see it or feel it,
If he wants it to be there."

— Flannery O'Connor

CHAPTER 9

Seminary, Early Years

On a hot, muggy day in late August, I entered Saint Paul Seminary. The campus is situated on the eastern banks of the Mississippi River. I was assigned a room in the recently constructed seminary residence and office building, which was attached to the old Saint Mary Chapel. We, a group of fifteen seminarians, were the second class to enjoy the new four-story structure. Some of the resident rooms faced south and overlooked a small creek, the library, and Bryne Residence for retired priests—the latter also newly built. The best accommodations were those on the west side since they provided a view of the Mississippi River and the Minneapolis skyline. Those who lived in the east and north quarters saw only a concrete courtyard, chapel, and seminary offices. A shower and toilet area joined every two resident rooms. This arrangement created the name "pottymate," which indicated that another seminarian shared a bathroom.

My assigned room was located on the third floor facing north. My "pottymate" was a third-year seminarian from the Archdiocese. His daily routine was to rise early in the morning, call his parents, and proceed to carry on a very noisy conversation. This annoyed me since this would often cause me to wake up—a nuisance I would endure for the entire year. One of my classmates, Bob, occupied a room across the hall, while the rest were scattered throughout the floors and wings.

The courses, like any other graduate college programs, were

held primarily in one building. I struggled in my theological lessons; yet, I succeeded in every class.

Our classes were held four days a week with the exception of Wednesday, which was set aside as a day of formation. The whole seminary student body participated in these mid-weekly morning rector conferences. A "rector" is the head of the seminary. These sessions included formation topics, such as how to sustain a balanced life of prayer, exercise, and work, and what were appropriate and healthy sexual boundaries.

During one of the talks, a classmate was granted permission to invite a Vincentian priest to speak about his priesthood. What this priest shared during that hour profoundly influenced my thinking about alcohol for the next twenty-plus years. He revealed to us that only the week before, he realized he had an addiction to alcohol. He said the first step of gaining control over his drinking (besides to stop drinking altogether) was to disclose his dependence on alcohol to our entire class.

A question that roamed inside of me for years after his talk, as I learned about Alcoholics Anonymous, concerned "a spiritual awakening." In my confusion, I thought to myself, *How could a priest have a spiritual awakening? Didn't they already have one?* It took years before I would grasp the difference between being spiritual and being religious. It would be several more years before this awareness would penetrate my heart, as my thinking was as slow as a turtle crossing a road.

Beginning the second semester, each first-year seminarian was given a teaching parish where they would be trained directly by a pastor. This experience was designed to offer the seminarian supervision and valuable feedback allowing the seminarian to reflect theologically on his experiences and identify his gifts of service and leadership within the church. Another beneficial piece of the program involved the formation of the Teaching Parish Committee to aid the seminarian, which was comprised of a group of diverse parishioners. The seminarians appointed to a teaching parish would remain there throughout their time in the seminary.

I was assigned to Corpus Christi Parish in Newport where the associate pastor was to be my supervisor. Between the time I learned about my teaching parish and the first time I drove to the parish, a variation developed. When I contacted the priest, who was to be my mentor, he informed me of his imminent transfer to another parish. Nonetheless, he agreed to meet with me in his office. As advised by another seminarian, I thought the trip to the parish would take about one-half hour. Unfortunately, I had not considered rush hour traffic, and the drive took me twice as long.

Once entering the church office, I was greeted by one of the ladies who worked there and asked for the priest. Louise let me know that the priest had left, since he believed that I'd opted not to come. She then introduced herself, informing me that she was the Pastoral Minister at the parish and that she would be my supervisor. My expression must have revealed my disappointment. Her face and tone of voice became sad and dejected as she inquired if I was okay having her as my teaching parish supervisor. She then invited me into her office so we could visit.

Even though I was disheartened to learn my mentor was a layperson instead of a priest-supervisor like the rest of my classmates, I soon realized what a warm, gentle, and compassionate spirit encompassed her heart. Louise was a caring, supportive, and effective mentor. I appreciated what she taught me about parish life and pastoral ministry. Ultimately, we would go on to have a superb mentor-student bond for the next three and a half years.

While having a positive and meaningful experience with my supervisor at Corpus Christi, I felt that I missed out on valuable lessons and the detailed reality about a typical day of a parish priest and pastor. Moreover, as in the circumstances throughout most of my life, I felt that I was shortchanged due to not being mentored by a male figure, as the pastor gave me little of his time.

Part of our priesthood formation mandated that first-year students submit an application to a Clinical Pastoral Education (CPE) program intended for the forthcoming summer. CPE is an interfaith professional education for ministry designed for theological students and ministers. Those who apply to this program are supervised both individually and in a group, and typically serve in a health-care setting. Through the practice of theological reflection on specific human conditions with a supervisor and with the group, one acquires a new understanding of ministry and develops skills in interpersonal and interprofessional relationships.

When the time came for me to apply for a CPE program, the dean of students summoned me into his office. A decision by the seminary formation team determined that I was not adequately mature relationally to participate in a CPE program; they wanted me to delay going until the following year. I was an introvert, quiet and shy. They didn't feel I would gain enough if I continued. They believed that I needed to be more outgoing.

What I always thought was the "norm" is not what the rest of society considers the "norm." At this point, I was insecure about whether I could be something I was not. Once again, I felt like I was a failure.

The dean recommended that I live in a parish rectory and work. Soon afterwards, I contacted the pastor of my home parish, Saint Vincent de Paul in Osseo, and asked if he had room for me to stay in his rectory over the summer. He did not. However, Father Curtis suggested that I might dwell in the vacant convent next door to the rectory.

The convent proved to be somewhat comfortable but very dusty, and I detected a few mice who also called the convent home. Despite this, I enjoyed my time there. I returned to my summer job at the Holiday Station Store nearby in Rogers and worked virtually full-time hours every week. Even so, I still managed to have some free time.

The highlight of the summer was writing letters and sending sports newspaper clippings each week to Bob, my fellow seminarian who had lived across the hall from me the prior year, and was staying in Oaxaca, Mexico, for the summer. Bob in turn wrote back each week sharing about his experiences.

Later that summer, a suicide overshadowed my family. One night my mom called to inform me of a friend's son who had hanged himself in the shower, leaving behind his two young children. Later, my sister Lori telephoned, expressing her disbelief and incomprehension of how anyone could take their own life. Lost for words, I struggled to console her, as this suicide was the first encounter I had with this manner of death.

Returning for the second year of my theological studies, our class structure shifted with two previous classmates pulling out and four seminarians joining the seminary, including two for the Archdiocese. I moved to the second floor facing south, now having an improved view of the landscape.

This school year was more or less a run-of-the-mill one, with nothing out of the ordinary. However, one of the new seminarians, Ray (from the Diocese of Cheyenne, Wyoming), and I would become friends, along with his pottymate, Tim, who also was preparing to be a priest in the Archdiocese. I continued my friendship from the previous year with Dave from the Diocese of Winona. Since we all lived on the same floor and wing, we spent a great deal of time together and our relationships deepened as a result.

Since I had not entered a CPE program the summer before, I now received the go-ahead to apply from the dean of studies. I submitted my application to Saint Mary's Medical Center in Duluth, Minnesota. Within a month, I received a letter indicating that I had been accepted to take part in their summer program.

Next, I needed to find my own housing. With some help, I quickly located a place to live for the summer. I acquired a room at Holy Family Catholic Church's rectory on the west side of Duluth. Later, I found out that I would be living with another seminarian who carpooled with me to Saint Mary's, and two other priests.

My summer in Duluth was an enjoyable one but passed by quickly. The CPC program with three other seminarians and two laypersons went well, although I continued to wrestle internally whenever I had to share my feelings. These feelings were a result of circumstances that occurred while calling on patients, and from an emergency encounter I experienced. One Friday night, I received a call to come to the hospital and be present when the doctor had to reveal to parents that their three-year-old son had died from drowning. The experience was one of the toughest ones I had that summer. I struggled to verbalize how I was feeling and why as well. Growing up, my family always kept their feelings to themselves, so I never saw anyone express themselves or witnessed how to work through emotions. I kept my feelings bottled up inside of me until finally, during a group session, I succumbed to my emotions. The thought of releasing the feelings that I had pent up had mortified me, but afterwards, I felt better. Even so, my ability to show my feelings did not become any easier throughout the remainder of summer.

CHAPTER 10

Seminary, Later Years

The CPE program ended in the middle of August, leaving me two weeks to prepare and make arrangements to study abroad. I was to visit Rome, Greece, and Jerusalem. Each fall, third-year theology students had the option of learning and living in the Holy Land. Tim and Ray joined me for the flight to Rome. Everything ran along smoothly. While in the Eternal City, we met up with our classmates Jim and Rodney. From Rome, we took a train ride to the coastal city of Bari, and a ferry to Greece. Our two groups became separated once reaching the Greek shores, but finally stumbled across each other as we embarked on another ferry for Haifa three days later. From the Israeli port city, we transferred to a bus that carried us to our destination. Once arriving in Jerusalem, we stayed for three and a half months at the Tantur Ecumenical Institute. Once there, we met four other classmates who were already present, along with our seminary faculty representative: our moral theology professor, Dr. Rose. Besides taking some courses with other partici-pants at the Institute and any ministers on sabbatical, we also trav-eled with them on short day outings and when touring northern Israel and the Sea of Galilee.

About three-fourths into our stay a critical conflict surfaced. Our seminary staff representative called a class meeting one after-noon to air things out. During this meeting, I had been extremely angry at Dr. Rose. I disliked feeling like she coddled us, treating us like schoolchildren rather than the young adults we were. As I shared my concern, my anger exploded. It was clear to me I still held within me much anger. If I were to be ordained, these feelings would require serious management. My angry outburst almost kept me from reaching my dream as a priest. I did not understand why I experienced these outbursts of anger and continued to feel different from others while burying inside the disappointment I had with myself.

Walking the land as Jesus did created fresh insights about the Gospels of Jesus, which continued with me to this day. Since we were residing in the Holy Land for several months, after a while we no longer felt like we were tourists. With this, we experienced more completely the day-to-day life of the Jewish society as well as the Palestinians. Some of us even shared meals within the homes of these Bethlehem residents. Attending the Sabbath and other Orthodox Christian and Catholic services filled up the majority of our time. When hearing about the violence between the two types of people on the news, the reports of injuries or killings are no longer just numbers, but are real and personal, striking within the depths of my heart.

The spring semester, like the previous year, finished up rather ordinary. The only extra undertaking was to figure out what to do with my free summer. Furthermore, the Dean of Students recommended that I apply to the Global Fellows Program (GFP), presented by Catholic Relief Services (CRS). This nonprofit organization considers itself the right arm of the American Catholic bishops who assist those around the world in need with aid, and in programs to support the underprivileged get out of their poverty. The GFP for seminarians was to have these future priests become aware of their service and operations so that once ordained as priests, they could be ambassadors for the organization.

That year, twenty seminarians around the United States, including myself, were introduced to the CRS mission via a two-week tour of Egypt and Burkino Faso in West Africa. Each week was devoted to each country learning about their work and the programs which sustained them.

We landed in Cairo and boarded a bus to take us to a Coptic Catholic seminary. Within the Catholic Church, there are twenty-four rites in union with the Pope. The Coptic Catholic eastern rite is one, while the majority of Catholic Christians belong to the Latin Rite or what is sometimes known as the Western Rite.

As we drove through Cairo, it seemed we would never arrive at the seminary. The endless road revealed a number of "living cemeteries," referring to the homeless, and these slums extended endlessly. I never saw such a substantial population existing in destitution and found it mind-boggling. Even the seminary was filled with impoverished seminarians whom we mingled with, and they were some of the highest-spirited people I have ever come across.

The next day, we traveled south along the Nile River to a city called Aswan. We stopped at a Coptic church and rectory where the priest and his wife greeted us at their door. Eastern Catholic–rite priests outside the United States may marry if accomplished before their priesthood ordination. They too dwelled in poverty; yet like the seminarians we visited the previous day, they were contented individuals.

I observed the identical attitude among the people in land-locked Burkino Faso, one of the poorest countries in the world, with insignificant products to export. Because of their scarcity of natural resources, foreign governments have negligible appeal to this Western African country, which renders CRS's presence even more valuable for its citizens. This element made our visit all the more influential to the seminarians, priests, and beneficiaries of CRS that we greeted.

An illustration of the impact CRS had happened in a village away from the capital city of Ouagadougou. While driving on the road, as we reached the edge of this community, almost all of the villagers approached us singing and playing native instruments. We sat outside a home learning about the services provided by CRS, such as giving loans to the women of the village, which gave them the financial means to create a product which she in turn sold for a profit. Eventually, they paid back the loan while also becoming capable of improving their lifestyle.

One of the questions I posed to a villager was, "Why did we receive that great welcoming when we arrived at their village?" She responded that they were grateful for Catholic Americans caring for them. They believed that we were proclaiming the Gospel that day, by our company and by the assistance of CRS. Moreover, in our coming to their village, they considered that Christ had come to them through our presence. This answer has lingered in my conscience, aware of how one's simple presence when being Christlike can create an immense impression on another individual.

Our fourth-year class composition again changed at the beginning of the new school year, with some leaving the seminary, and others joining. This would be the year of making the commitment to be ordained the following spring. The seminary faculty as well as our teaching parish supervisors evaluated us, and then submitted a recommendation to the rector of the seminary. My previous confrontation at that class meeting with the faculty member while in the Holy Land came back to haunt me.

Before endorsing my priesthood ordination, Dr. Rose had written her serious reservations about my becoming a priest, suggesting that I go to counseling to work through my anger problems. Having examined her concerns, the rector required that I attend counseling sessions before decreeing a final decision and his blessing to the Archbishop, who had the ultimate voice in ordaining me.

Consequently, I proceeded to go to therapy meetings at the University of Saint Thomas counseling center for anger management and relationship development skills. After three sessions, the counselor came to the conclusion that I was psychologically competent to be a priest, as he thought I was a normal, average individual. He found nothing "wrong with me."

With this judgement of my personality, the rector forwarded his affirmative recommendation to my Archbishop.

All seminarians enter into holy orders of the Catholic Church with their ordination to the deaconate, if transitional, and what follows is the priesthood. Some men enter into the deaconate permanently without seeking the priesthood and can be married, but if their wife dies before him, he cannot remarry. Once becoming a transitional deacon, he becomes a member of the clergy, which means that he now is required to remain celibate and obedient to their bishop and his successors.

On December 4, 1993, along with seven of my classmates, we were ordained deacons by Bishop Lawrence Welch, an auxiliary bishop of the Archdiocese of Saint Paul and Minneapolis at Saint Mary Seminary Chapel. My mom, my sister Lori and her husband and son, members of my teaching parish committee, and my supervisor joined in the ceremony and reception that followed. Joy permeated that mild winter day in Saint Paul for all of my family and friends who were present for the festivities.

Apprehensively, the next weekend at Corpus Christi, my legs shaking and palms sweating, I proclaimed my first homily at all the Sunday Masses. With the completion of the last weekend Mass, I nervously celebrated my first three baptisms. Pleased that I'd made it through my first preaching experience and baptisms, I eagerly drove back to the seminary where some of my classmates would gather sharing stories about our new ministry.

Overall, throughout the seminary, my drinking continued to be moderate without binges and only a few sporadic nights of heavy consumption. I was beginning to purchase a bottle more frequently. From time to time, I woke up with a hangover and splitting headache. At this time and bearing no other consequences, I still found myself able to function ordinarily in the morning. Nonetheless, I questioned for the first time if I was drinking too much. One night while ingesting sips from a bottle of Jim Beam, a knock came to the door. Resting the open container on my dresser, I opened the door to find a classmate asking for something. Waiting at the door, he had a direct view of the bottle. I was convinced he saw the open Jim Beam and must have smelled alcohol on my breath; however, he never mentioned it.

During that school year, two parties took place where alcohol was present. I lied about who was paying for the several bottles of alcohol supplied at the two class gatherings. I would buy an assortment of alcohol, around eight to ten bottles, and when asked who provided it, I informed them that it was my pastor. After the party, I would take the unused portions to my room, where over the next months I would empty them out completely.

For Christmas break, I traveled to Garden City where preparations for my priesthood ordination were to begin. A group of Mom's church friends, along with me, created a bulky scrapbook of my life. While working on this autobiographical album, seeing pictures of my birth father and other photos, my eyes filled with tears. Afterwards, as well as in the years to follow, I often pondered how my life might possibly have been altered after my birth dad had been tragically killed that fateful night.

While in my hometown, I celebrated the tasks assigned to a deacon at the midnight Christmas Mass at Saint Dominic along with another deacon. I still hold warm memories of that first Christmas as a clergyman.

A few months later, I took part in the Holy Week services at Saint Lawrence Catholic Campus Center at the University of Kansas. The highlight of being a deacon was participating in the ritual observances of Jesus' Last Supper, passion, death, and resurrection. Seeing college students enter into the ceremonies with such fervor and faith conveyed the impression on me of the depth of faith these young adults encompassed.

Concluding the Easter Vigil Mass, Father Vince, his associate pastor, and I returned to the rectory for a strong martini as we reminisced about the splendor of the evening—a tradition I maintained for numerous years. When they left for their bedroom, I made myself another drink and took it to the privacy of my room.

The next day I set out for Minnesota. The freshness of spring in eastern Kansas saturated the air. My faith in Jesus Christ was reaffirmed as I intensely felt Jesus Christ's resurrection throughout my journey to the north. Smiles often formed on my face when thinking about the past days spent in Lawrence.

Upon returning to Saint Paul, only six weeks remained before my ordination into the priesthood. There were final oral exams to cram for. Waiting in preparation for this momentous event to arrive absorbed excessive amounts of my time during those final days at the seminary.

Invitations needed to be mailed, ordination and First Mass receptions required finalization, and worship aids for the celebrations needed to be proofed. Arrangements for the immediate family as well as some extended family members were completed.

The most significant date that year, besides the day of the ordination in May, happened during the middle of that month. Together with my seven other Archdiocesan classmates, we received an invitation from our vocation director to join him for lunch at a nearby restaurant. None of us really cared about the meal itself, since what we would be finding out was far more valuable.

Eagerly, we entered the restaurant, sat down, and ordered our meal. Then the moment we had been waiting for arrived. The vocation director strolled around our table, stopping at each of our places, giving us one by one an envelope with our name on it. We knew that inside of the envelope was a letter from Archbishop Roach informing us where our first assignment was as a parish priest. I had no indication which parish I would be sent to. The letter read: "Fr. Wasinger, I hereby appoint you as parochial vicar of the Church of Saint Pius X, White Bear Lake, Minnesota, effective noon on June 22, 1994."

Additionally, in the letter, it acknowledged that each of our names would be published in the next issue of *The Catholic Register*—the official newspaper of the Archdiocese of Saint Paul and Minneapolis. Finally, I was feeling like I was accepted by my peers and was so excited to be a part of this great group! When the paper arrived in my mailbox the succeeding week, all of my classmates' names and parish assignments were in it, excluding mine. I called the Archdiocese to let them know my name was missing from the paper. A faint apology was offered with assurances that my name would be in the next issue. In the subsequent issue, I began searching for my name, which again was not included. Finally, in the ensuing issue my assignment was mentioned. What I presumed would be a one-time occurrence would tend to create a pattern of lack of acknowledgement which has persisted to the present day.

Over time, this and other incidents created a feeling of great insig-
nificance within my being. A part of me wishes that I had checked
into why these mistakes had been made. Instead, I quietly stuffed
down my disappointments, burying them deep with so many other
unanswered questions.

Since I had never been to the Church of Saint Pius X, in suburban Saint Paul, the following day I drove off to explore and familiar-
ize myself with the surroundings. I drove around it but did not stop
to go inside. The next Sunday, I showed up incognito for Mass.

Ten days before my priesthood ordination, I flew west to
Monterrey, California, where my Uncle Emmanuel, a religious
brother, waited to pick me up. Eager to meet my uncle, I immediately spotted him after arriving at the gate. Even though it was the
first time ever seeing my dad's younger brother, he looked a lot
like my dad. After he joined this California religious house in the
early 1960s, Brother Emmanuel never returned to Kansas, keeping
us from ever meeting previously.

In an old ramshackle truck, we traveled south on California
Highway 1, along the Pacific Ocean shores, through the small town
of Big Sur to Immaculate Heart of Mary Camaldolese Hermitage.
As stunning as the view was from the road, to view from the top of
the two-mile climb up the mountain was even more breathtaking.
Looking down onto the ocean, the landscape was phenomenal. The
water glistened as if it was being kissed by the sun. My guest room
overlooking the Pacific Ocean amidst this peaceful, quiet setting
filled my heart with contentment.

During the week, Brother Emmanuel drove me in an old golfing
cart everywhere on the hermitage's property. One day my uncle
informed me that we would be going farther up the mountain to
chop wood. He asked me to assist him in splitting the wood. He

would swing the ax, as I placed the wood onto the trailer which was hooked to the cart. Twenty minutes later I complained about being tired.

"I need a break," I said, frustrated. My uncle, thirty-five years older, replied with a smirk, "What? We are just getting started! Aren't you a farm boy?" With that, he continued to cut wood for another two hours in silence.

At the hermitage, the monks gathered together in their distinctive chapel. One section was oblong, chairs and pews facing the center from both sides, the presider's chair at one side and the ambo at the opposite side: this area was used for prayer and for the Liturgy of the Word, or the first part of a Catholic Mass. Behind the ambo, a large concrete circle made up the space, the altar at its center; it was utilized for the Liturgy of the Eucharist, or second half of a service.

The monks and any guests assembled numerous times each day for prayer, Mass, and Adoration of the Holy Eucharist. I joined the Masses and some of the prayer periods; however, I never showed up in the morning because I desired to sleep in. When leaving to go home, Brother Emmanuel, while saying good-bye, communicated his disenchantment in my not attending the morning services. I felt the choice I made had hurt my uncle, in that his nephew, soon to be a priest, had not been as prayerful as he'd expected. Disappointing him caused me to be ashamed and angry at myself for not doing what was expected of me.

A fellow monk, along with another guest and I, were chauffeured back to Monterrey's airport. Flying back to Minnesota, only three days remained before the greatest day in my life.

CHAPTER 11

Ordination

Jubilation filled the air as a small number of family members began to land at Minneapolis–Saint Paul airport. The preceding evening of the ordination, we gathered for a family dinner at my brother-in-law's aunt and uncle's home in Maplewood. We sat outside on a warm Minnesota evening free of mosquitoes. We chatted and chuckled as tales were told about my growing up, such as when I tumbled into a bucket of broken glass cutting my elbow, needing stitches, resulting in a permanent scar. My cousin Tina, who was present, shared about playing "Mass" in our youth. The evening was bursting with memories.

The next morning, May 28, 1994, one of the most significant days in my life, had finally arrived. Before departing from the seminary, my seven classmates and I gathered into the first-floor communal space for Morning Prayer. Afterwards, Mom (who was staying in the seminary guest room) and I walked from one end of Saint Paul's famous tree-lined Summit Avenue to the other end, to the grandiose Cathedral of Saint Paul which is positioned on the top of a hill above downtown Saint Paul and the Mississippi River.

The massive Cathedral of Saint Paul is one of the largest in the United States; the First Eucharistic service was celebrated in 1915, yet it was not completed until the 1950s. When my two-year-old nephew Tyler saw the inside, he shouted, "Big, big, big!" as he pointed up with his finger. My few family members, teaching parish committee, and some other friends sat near the front in the reserved seating section. We were a large ordination class by the standards of the day, and our family and friends virtually packed the cathedral, which could accommodate 3,000 souls within its pews for our Mass of Ordination.

My classmates and I walked in the procession for Mass and were seated in the first row, left of the aisle. The ceremony presided by the Archbishop John Roach, spiritual leader of the Archdiocese of Saint Paul and Minneapolis, began promptly at 10:00 a.m. and continued for two hours. After the homily, my peers and I received Holy Orders when the Archbishop laid his hands on each of us and anointed us with the Sacred Chrism oils. Then we joined the Archbishop for the first time around the altar for the Eucharistic Prayer, where Catholics believe the bread and wine are transformed into the real Body and Blood of Christ—an astounding mystery of our faith.

At the end of the Mass, a deacon announced that the newly ordained would be on the south-side lawn where we could give our first blessings as a priest and pose with others for pictures. We proceeded after the recession in our vestments to our spots outside the cathedral, into the blazing sun, high humidity, unseasonably hot, windless day. Immediately sweating in the 93-degree temperature, I could not wait to take off my religious wardrobe and get into my air-conditioned car.

A light reception of punch, coffee, and cake followed at Saint Leonard of Port Maurice Church in South Minneapolis. The previous summer, I had interned at that African-American parish. Even though the underground room was not air-conditioned, it was far more comfortable than standing outside.

Commonly, however not in all instances, a newly ordained priest is given a chalice by his family or one that has been passed down from a previous family priest who has died. On the bottom of my chalice is inscribed "Love Joe and Betty." This couple, members of my teaching parish, were compassionate, big-hearted, and welcoming; it was in their home where we held our teaching parish committee meetings. Their gesture of presenting me with my first chalice showed how much they love me and their Catholic faith.

The following afternoon, I celebrated my First Mass at my "home" parish of Saint Vincent de Paul in Osseo. Yet again, it was miserably hot since the AC was turned down following an earlier Mass. Anxious now, particularly since it was hot, I listened to the music for Mass to get underway. Suddenly, I became flustered as I was not ready to start! Providentially, my friend Ray, who thankfully served as the deacon at Mass, was with me in the sacristy assisting getting me dressed and was able to calm me down.

When I turned the switch on the cordless microphone I was wearing, it did not work. A handheld mic nearby was handed to Ray, who supported it in front of me as I began the religious service. Father Stan, ordained two years earlier, preached a homily on the Holy Trinity—the theme for that Sunday. With the exception of having to tolerate the heat, the remainder of Mass progressed on without any snags.

A dinner reception at a local hotel ballroom completed the festivities of the weekend. For the three following weekends, I also celebrated Masses of Thanksgiving. The first two I celebrated at my teaching parish, and the last one in the parish where I had aided the pastor the prior summer.

I flew to Kansas for two more events and Masses—first at the church of my Confirmation in Garden City and then the next day at the church of my First Holy Communion in Scott City. Many friends of my mom and dad attended the Mass at Saint Dominic. Only Grandma Stoppel and a few other relatives of my birth father came to the service. Not until years later did I understand why other family members had not been present at that Mass. My birth father's name was not cited on the invitations or any of the news media; only my second dad had been mentioned. Looking back, I wish I had thought to place my birth father's name on everything as with my other dad that adopted me.

The last Mass of Thanksgiving was offered at Saint Joseph Church with a reception to follow. I relished reconnecting with family and friends from my time on the farm, some of whom I had not seen in years. My sister Kyra, husband Larry, and nephews Erron and Evan were in attendance. Erron, thirteen at the time, sat close to me and was mischievous at the event. While I was looking away and talking with someone during the reception, he poured salt into my water. Later, I took a sip, instinctively spitting out the water, causing those around to look at me. An embarrassing moment was followed by a shared smile with my nephew.

Once all of the gatherings were finished in Kansas, it was time to return to Minnesota to pack my remaining belongings at the seminary and move into my first rectory, located at the Church of Saint Pius X.

CHAPTER 12

First Assignment

S aint Pope Pius X Catholic Church of White Bear Lake, Minnesota, was founded in 1954. The former Holy Father was canonized earlier that year and soon after the church was built. The offices, social hall, and worship spaces were extended and remodeled in 1992, two years prior to my arrival. The ranch-style rectory was located a short distance from the main church structure.

The parish administrative and pastoral center consisted of the reception area and four offices facing out towards the parking lot. My office was sandwiched between the pastor and business administrator. Since this was the first office I ever enjoyed as my own, I eagerly began to organize it. Just as I started setting some of my books and knickknacks on the bookshelf, the pastor, Father Mike, popped his head inside the door.

"Don't you want to paint your office first?" my pastor pointed out.

"Can I?" I replied, surprised.

"Yes, any color within reason," came back the response.

"Thanks," I answered.

We discussed the details, and within a week, my new office was freshly painted. I once again placed books and other possessions on the book ledges. I hung my items on the walls, including a framed picture with the saying, "Shepherding each other"—an ordination gift from one of my classmates. Each time I walked by the mounted quote, I was reminded how every Christian is called to minister to one another whether they are a priest, a religious brother or sister, or a layperson. Throughout my priesthood, numerous parishioners have been my personal "shepherd" by actions—their acts of compassion, words of encouragement, and support.

My next task was to arrange my bedroom and sitting room which were located on the west side of the rectory. My comfortable, sizeable, sunlit bedroom in the northwest corner of the home provided a beautiful view of the next-door neighbor's yard, lavish with trees to the west, while the view north overlooked a synthetic pond surrounded by fifteen or so houses.

As with my office, Father Mike encouraged the painting of the bedroom and sitting-room areas. Creatively, the top half of the wall was painted a light blue, the bottom half a darker blue, with the middle a wallpaper border. I spartanly decorated the rooms with minimal furnishings and wall hangings.

Less than one month after becoming a priest, I presided over my first funeral Mass, that of my Grandma Wasinger. Her service would be held at Saint Dominic in Garden City. Not only was I anxious about being the celebrant of the Mass and preaching a homily in front of family, but I was tense over the presence of the pastor, who instructed me to carry out the funeral service in his style, not in the way I had been instructed in the seminary. Despite this, the funeral Mass went well and without any issues.

By this time, I had settled into parish life and was waiting for the school year to begin. Saint Pius X Parish ran a school from kindergarten to eighth grade. From time to time, I would go and visit with the students in their classrooms, ask them questions, and answer any questions they might have for me. I also taught religion classes to raucous eighth-graders once a week.

In the fall, Father Mike requested that I, along with Rachel, our new Director of Religious Education, develop a Rite of Christian Initiation (RCIA). The curriculum's purpose was to educate people on our faith and spiritually. It also was to form those who sought to be baptized into, or wanted to join, the Catholic Church. Some wanted to convert from another religion, while others needed to complete their formation in the Catholic faith so as to be confirmed.

Rachel and I team-taught, each of us teaching the subject themes that interested us the most. The subjects I taught were on the lives of the saints, the history of the Catholic Church, and the Sacraments. The RCIA sessions began in October and concluded at the Easter Vigil, which was the time each person would be entirely initiated into the Catholic Church.

The adult pastoral social ministry had a similar program for the youth of the parish. Ten students ages 14 to 18 participated in the youth pastoral social ministry organized by our pastoral minister, Mary. One of the first teens that Mary introduced me to was a skinny fourteen-year-old named Doug. He, along with his two closest friends, participated in the ministry group throughout their four years of high school. Doug and I became friends and have sustained our friendship for twenty-five years.

There were two priests for the 1,600-household parish, and all but the administrative obligations, which ordinarily were the responsibilities of the pastor, were shared and fluctuated each day of the week. Father Mike urged me to get away from the parish on my free day for my emotional and spiritual health. A majority of the time I would spend my day off with my classmate Tim, and we would do a variety of activities together. There were also days when I would stay around the rectory, reading or accomplishing other tasks at hand.

Early on, I found parish life as a priest at Saint Pius X surprisingly not very demanding. Father Mike's and my pastoral ministry work was fairly divided between us, so the biggest challenge at that time was learning how to work with the parish staff and trying to remember all the names of the parishioners, the latter being exceptionally problematic. This happened for two reasons. First, I have a hard time recalling names unless I've had an important encounter with a person, and second, I was very shy and afraid to ask anyone to repeat their name. Many years later, I came to realize that not calling a parishioner by name when talking with them might appear as if I had little concern for them. This, however, was far from the case.

Even though newly ordained priests may have all the book-knowledge of how to observe sacraments and pastoral affairs, celebrating sacraments in a caring and placid manner is another story. For example, during my Saint Paul Seminary formation, I fostered a passion for the liturgy, mainly since our liturgy professor, Father Bonaventure, conveyed his obvious enthusiasm for Catholic worship. I shared with him an article that I wrote in the parish bulletin about some aspect of the Mass which was more about following the letter of the law than being pastoral in carrying out a ritual, which was much to his displeasure.

Another pastoral responsibility delegated to me was to prepare couples for impending marriages. Due to an oversight, the previous pastor had reserved three Matrimonial Masses for the same Saturday in September. However, the parish's schedule allowed for only two marriage ceremonies to occur on any specific Saturday. I ended up performing the third couple's ceremony at the neighboring parish of Saint Jerome in Maplewood.

During the homily, I shared with the couple, John and Pam Stuber, that we were "green" in what we were doing—they a newly married couple, and myself a newly ordained priest. We all shared a chuckle at this fact, and this was something that we would continue to bring up from time to time when we saw each other.

As destiny would have it, when I moved to North Branch ten years after their wedding, I found that John and Pam Stuber also lived in North Branch and were parishioners of the parish I was assigned to, Saint Gregory the Great. Having earlier buried Pam's father and baptized their firstborn daughter, we reconnected. Since I've lived in North Branch, I have baptized their youngest daughter, celebrated all three of their children's First Communions, and was present at their two oldest children's Confirmations. One of the most meaningful and satisfying attributes of being a priest is becoming a "family priest" to those families who have welcomed me to be a part of their lives. I've also become a family priest to the Winds from Saint Pius X, and more recently, the Graffs from Saint Gregory the Great.

This aspect of the priesthood is particularly valuable to me. Within my own family, I have not celebrated many sacraments. In fact, on my mother's side of the family, I have only been part of my immediate family's celebrations of baptisms and First Communions, but no sacraments of Confirmation or Matrimony. On the Stoppel and Wasinger sides of the family, I have only performed a few weddings and baptisms. This is the reason why I treasure my time spent with other families.

Besides acquiring experience and wisdom on how to excel in pastoral ministry, I benefited from Larry, the business administrator of the parish. In my opinion, Larry was a brilliant and sagacious employee. Not only was he knowledgeable about business aspects of managing a parish, but he was excellent at mentoring his expertise in this area. This was one of the paramount talents he would pass on to me. Even after I left the parish, for years I continued to call upon him, receiving his guidance on legal and business matters pertaining to the church. I was privileged to work alongside Larry for four years and will forever be indebted to him.

Many other close friendships with families were fostered during my years in White Bear Lake. I continue my connection with these parishioners, some more so than others. Although not their family priest, the Carr, Sonntag, and Zech families lived close to the rectory and I would become friends with all of them. The Carrs' fine-looking yard and house faced my bed- and sitting rooms. I would wander over from time to time for spur-of-the moment visits. The Sonntags, who were close to Father Mike, would also invite me to their home, and I even enjoyed a few holidays with their family.

The street in front of the rectory split into a fork. The Zech family lived on the first plot with land on either side of the two streets. Because of their location, when walking to the church, from time to time I passed through their lawn. Customarily, one or all of the five children would be playing outside on the grass, and I found myself at times joining in on whatever sporting activity they were enjoying.

Gina, the middle child, would become the first female altar server at Saint Pius X, serving with her brother Tony. I considered her like a niece, as I did with the rest of her siblings. One day Nick, the oldest, invited me to celebrate Mass at Hill-Murray, the local Catholic high school he attended. My experience presiding at that Mass with hundreds of teenagers would lead to the beginning of my ministry with high-schoolers.

The Thompsons lived the greatest distance away from the

church. Even so, they often invited me to their home where the wife and mother, Connie, always cooked a fantastic meal. One of the highlights I had with this family was being introduced to each of their three youngest daughters' future husbands during one of these meals. Another household I remained close with is the Lee family. The middle son of their three children, Jeff, asked me to be his Confirmation sponsor—an honor that I readily accepted.

After my first year in White Bear Lake, my mom left Garden City, Kansas. Packing her possessions as well as her furniture, she moved to Hopkins, Minnesota, located on the west side of the Minneapolis and Saint Paul Metro Area. She rented an apartment and enrolled in a two-year CPE program at Methodist Hospital in neighboring Saint Louis Park.

Grateful that Mom lived close to me, I relished her company. Having family close by was important to me as this allowed a comfortable place where I could just be myself. As a priest, there is a certain standard we place upon ourselves, behaving in a certain way, trying to say the right thing, even though sometimes you would like to scream! I welcomed the chance to get things off my chest. Besides being less than an hour away, it also gave me a chance to appreciate her cooking, notably her fried chicken and cube steak with gravy, which are my favorites! Every time I attempted to make gravy; it was never as scrumptious as hers. Mom traveled over to White Bear for visits, and we would occasionally meet at the Mall of America in Bloomington for lunch. Residing in Minnesota ended when she decided to relocate to Grand Junction, Colorado, to be near to my sister Lori who'd recently given birth to her third child, Keenan.

In addition to having living quarters upstairs in the rectory, I also enjoyed using the sizeable downstairs living room which had a fireplace and a walkout to the pond in the backyard. Practically every night and on weekends when I was free from meetings or other activities, I sat in the room watching television. The space provided a cool, comfortable spot during the hot summer months, and in the winter the fireplace created a cozy, warm environment.

The living room also served as an ideal setting to drink alcohol in the evening. At first, I hid bottles of vodka upstairs in my bedroom closet, going up a time or two each evening to fill my tumbler of alcohol and orange pop. With my pastor's room just five feet from the basement door, just to be safe, I would cover my cup with tinfoil so the aroma would not emerge. When the other priest was away, I would bring the vodka and soft drink downstairs.

My vodka drinking now occurred most evenings, starting at 6:30 p.m. and continuing to 10:20 p.m. when the TV weather forecast was finished. As I headed to bed, more often than not I was intoxicated. I would usually wake up in the morning with a mild hangover. My addiction had not yet produced any problems in the morning or at work. Still, I became troubled over how much and how frequently I was drinking. I would often question myself repeatedly in my mind if this was indeed a problem, even though no one around me suggested that it was.

I spoke with Father Mike one day, during my fourth year at Saint Pius, about my drinking. We chatted for an hour, ending with his recommendation that I speak with another priest in the Archdiocese who supported those with an alcohol dependency. Immediately I contacted the priest, Matthew, whom I knew from Archdiocesan gatherings, to arrange a time for us to meet. I drove over to his parish two days later to disclose the alarm I was experiencing over my consumption of alcohol.

Matt opened our meeting by inquiring about the cause and asked for an account of my addiction. I revealed to him that my increase in drinking started when I worked in Monticello and I would come home from work and drink in order to fall asleep. He advised me that alcohol might help one fall asleep but would later cause poor sleeping patterns. I then recounted to Matt how much and how often I was drinking vodka. I also shared that I drank out of boredom and loneliness, and my desire to experience my feelings in a deeper manner since I was incapable of doing so in any of my relationships.

Once I finished speaking, he said he believed that the amount and frequency of my drinking indicated a problem. Matt keenly encouraged me to seek treatment and said he would assist me. I declined! As I left his office, Matthew asserted that one day alcoholism would catch up with me in a vile way.

At the time, while I was honest about my use of alcohol to Matt, I refused to pursue added support for my addiction. I thought I only had a problem with alcohol, not that I was an alcoholic. Moreover, how could I be one when there were no issues in my work or in my relationships? I held on to this belief for years, not able to accept the truth of my addiction.

Ordinarily, a newly ordained priest can expect to have one or two assignments that last two to five years before being assigned to a parish as the pastor or parochial administrator. Forty or fifty years ago, a priest might become an associate pastor for twenty years or so until receiving a pastorate. Today, a freshly ordained reverend can anticipate being assigned to his own parish community after one or two assignments.

My appointment at Saint Pius X lasted four years. In the spring of 1998, I was requested to consider a move to another parish, serving as a pastor. The Priests' Personnel Board—the group who in our Archdiocese recommends an individual to be appointed to a specific parish—suggested that I reflect on going to a midsize parish in the western suburbs on the shores of Lake Minnetonka.

Thus, the following weekend, along with some parishioners, I set off to that parish for Mass. Later in the week, I spoke with their pastor about the details of the parish. Since I'd felt right at home the previous Sunday and liked the comments of the pastor, I informed Father Mike, who was on the personnel board, that I wished to be sent to that church community.

As soon as I shared this with my pastor, he regrettably revealed that the personnel board requested another priest be recommended to that parish. The priest had accepted the assignment. I was no longer being considered. Initially I was understandably disappointed, not so much about not being assigned to this parish, but more so because I was not the right "fit" and they chose someone else. The right fit? Not this again! Why would they request of me to look at that parish if they were going to assign it to someone else?

At this time in my life, I don't believe they understood I was dependent on alcohol—at least it wasn't brought to my attention. Trusting them or what someone would say to me became more and more difficult. I didn't look forward to being set up for disappointment. Consequently, keeping my distance from others was something I was becoming good at. After all, you can't get hurt if you don't let people get too close.

Two months went by after this experience. As the summer came closer, I had yet to receive another assignment. This is, until the last week of May.

CHAPTER 13

Second Assignment

On the last Friday of May, I drove into Saint Paul to meet with Archbishop Harry Flynn and the Director of the Priests' Personnel Board, Father Samuel, to learn about my next assignment. When I arrived at the chancery, the Director greeted me carrying a sheet of paper. He asked me to wait in the reception area so he could first speak to Archbishop Flynn.

He then came back to tell me that we could now meet with the Archbishop. When I entered the office, the Archbishop and I briefly exchanged pleasantries. Holding the sheet that Samuel previously had, the Archbishop uttered, "I would like to appoint you to Saint Boniface and Saints Cyril and Methodius in northeast Minneapolis as the parochial administrator and as the chaplain at Academy of Holy Angels in Richfield, Minnesota, effective July 1, 1998."

I was shocked. Although I had expressed earlier that month to Father Samuel that I would like to be a high school chaplain, these parishes were not even on my radar.

"Oh" was the only word I could muster back to the Archbishop.

"This will be a good assignment for you, Father Shane," he assured me.

After fifteen minutes of discussion between the three of us, I timidly agreed to Archbishop Flynn's request. I could have said no, but I respected the Archbishop's wisdom, so I agreed with his decision. After all, I had consented to a vow of obedience to my "bishop and his successors" on my ordination day. As is customary, disclosing this new appointment was not allowed until I received a confirmation letter. In most circumstances, a priest will often tell a priest friend or two and some family members about his new assignment. I shared my information with my pastor. Once receiving the letter, I informed the parishioners at Saint Pius X the following Friday, June 5, at Mass—the feast day of Saint Boniface.

Three days later, I drove to Academy of Holy Angels in Richfield to visit with the principal and the campus ministers with which I would be working. We discussed what I might teach and my other duties, which would include celebrating all school Masses during the school year. The chaplain position was part-time with the expectation that I would teach two days a week. At the end of the meeting, the principal showed me my new office. A prior water leak had resulted in its somewhat poor condition and rank odor—a condition I would endure the remaining months and into the following school year.

I was not at all familiar with Saint Boniface Church and Saints Cyril and Methodius. All I knew at the time was their location in northeast Minneapolis, a geographic area recognized for many Catholic and Orthodox churches—the highest concentration in the Twin Cities. I visited the Slavic parish named after two brothers and toured the old rectory and church. Seven blocks south of Saints Cyril and Methodius, and on the same street, stood Saint Boniface's church and rectory.

I chose to attend Mass there one weekday morning to speak with the pastor about the parish and perhaps be granted a tour as well. Walking up to the front of the church I discovered the doors were locked. As I began to walk around the grounds, the church maintenance man and only employee, Larry, instructed me to go through the unlocked doors on the southeast side. As I walked to my pew, I felt inept, as all of the ten parishioners present were much older than me.

Once Mass was over, I went into the sacristy to visit the pastor, Father Odilo, a Benedictine monk from Saint John's Abbey in Collegeville, Minnesota. The monastery's fathers founded this originally German church in the mid-nineteenth century a few blocks from the Mississippi River. The present-day church structure was finished and dedicated in 1929 after years of being a mere basement building. This church was built to seat one-thousand souls. On the south side a story-high stained-glass window depicted the life of their patron saint. Numerous confessionals lined either side of the church, although only one was used. The marble communion rail remained in place but was no longer utilized since the changes of the Second Vatican Council of 1962–1965.

While in the sacristy, the pastor and I stood chatting about the parish. Fr. Odilo revealed that Saint Boniface parishioners continued to dwindle throughout the years. With a less significant population, the finances to run the parish were becoming more and more of a challenge. He conveyed his thoughts that the parish would have to close in five years. His remark definitely was not promising. In a month's time, I was to come to Saint Boniface Parish with little hope for its survival according to the current pastor. This left me feeling appalled regarding my first pastorate. Disheartened, I left without even requesting to see the rectory.

Since I had planned a vacation with my classmates Ray and Tim at the end of June to the first of July to Oregon and Washington, I raised the possibility of moving all of my possessions to the rectory before setting off on the trip with Fr. Odilo. He agreed. I brought my initial load of boxes over to Minneapolis some days later. As I walked into the priest's residence, I was greeted with a terrible stench. The main floor reeked of cigarette smoke, and the smell was intensified by the humidity. Dealing with this unexpected situation would have to be delayed until I returned from my trip.

The process of settling in and removing that smoky odor were my priorities upon my return. The condition of the rectory indicated that the occupants left in quite a hurry. When I walked into the kitchen, I could see the sink was crammed with dirty dishes, and the coffeepot was still half full. Lying on the dining-room table was an open copy of the *Minneapolis Star-Tribune* newspaper, an ashtray filled with ashes, and a partially used cigarette. For a moment I seriously thought about moving into the Saints Cyril and Methodius rectory, but then decided I'd see what I could do to fix up the house.

This mammoth rectory resembled a mansion. For years it had housed priests and brothers from Saint John's Abbey, essentially turning it into a mini monastery. The Benedictines had served in Saint Boniface Parish since its establishment in 1858, except during the American Civil War when diocesan priests ministered to the community. The transition of the parish from being served by Benedictine priests to a diocesan priest had proved to be an ordeal for both the parishioners and myself. The community was used to the style of ministry offered by the monks throughout the years. Before long, however, the parishioners adapted to my form of leadership, which was inspired by my time at the Benedictine monks of Conception Abbey and aided by my German ancestry.

Since the rectory was so large, I had a number of options as far as how to utilize the space in the building. There were a variety of rooms and office spaces within the two-story, full-basement priest's residence. Upstairs, the options included five bedrooms, two with adjoining sitting rooms, along with a private bathroom. I chose my bedroom to be located in the former housekeeper's quarters on the northeast second-floor side that had a living room and a nearby bathroom, along with its own staircase. For short-term purposes, one of the other bedrooms on the floor became my office and later became a chapel once the remodeling was finished on the main level. In addition to the kitchen and dining room on the ground floor were two bathrooms, a living room, pantry, entrance-way, and three offices with a twelve-foot-wide hallway, just like on the second floor.

Making headway unloading and organizing my bedroom and upstairs office, I began to clean up the first-floor disarray I had dis-covered in the former pastor's office and bedroom, which were both soiled and cluttered. A few days passed and amidst all the chaos, I began searching and searching for the parish checkbook to pay some bills; however, I could not locate it anywhere. Frustrated upon looking for the checkbook for over two hours, I telephoned the neighboring pastor, his church a block away, asking if he could come over soon to assist in my endeavor to uncover it. He obliged, arriving shortly. Father Joe needed little time to comb the office and discover the checkbook under a pile of papers—a spot I had checked over at least two or three times.

Sadly, in the first months of my pastorate at Saint Boniface, I was unable to get in touch with the previous pastor to get from him any answers about the parish or where items were located in the office. At first the lack of guidance was daunting; nevertheless, I proceeded to make the best out of the circumstances.

Since I did not live at Saints Cyril and Methodius' rectory and my office was at Saint Boniface for both parishes, the main presence at this church community encompassed celebrating Mass on two weekdays and every other weekend, attending meetings, and sign-ing checks. Thankfully, an old-timer efficiently managed the day-to-day dealings of the parish, allowing me more time with the other parish.

Also, I was blessed to employ a sacramental assistant who served at both parishes. Sacramental assistants are priests that provide for the parish their priestly services by celebrating Mass, baptisms, and other sacraments. Father John, a religious order priest, a former high school teacher, and retired, started his ministry at each parish when I arrived the past July.

Some of the parishioners, Father John, and myself engaged in a working Liturgy Committee, and its members seriously assumed their duties. Music and special liturgical observances such as Advent, Lent, and Holy Week were meticulously studied, planned, and incorporated into the parish services. I never had to concern myself with the quality of our liturgical services and Masses because of the dedication and faithfulness of this committee's members.

The third part of my appointment as chaplain at Academy of Holy Angels was to begin July 1st of that summer. For the first six weeks, there was very little to be done at the school except for a few meetings to aid in preparations for the new school year. Once mid-August rolled around, I started driving to Richfield, which entailed traveling through Minneapolis—a drive I detested—three half days a week. My duties were few: celebrate Mass once a week, participate in the campus ministry classes, be present for some spiritual needs of staff or students as requested, and lead a prayer before each varsity football game on Friday nights.

One of the highlights of my time spent at Holy Angels transpired at all our school Masses, which were celebrated at Saint Peter's Church across the parking lot. Students from the Campus Ministry class, along with their two teachers and me, arranged and carried out the liturgies. At most of these Masses, I would invite three or four pupils in advance to assist me in delivering the homily. They would stand in front of the church as I asked the questions we had discussed prior to Mass. In order, they typically would present the appropriate answers, although sometimes in a humorous way.

Unfamiliar with the high school football players, I felt apprehensive and awkward even conducting the short prayer before games and struggled to find the precise words to deliver in front of these teenage boys. After saying the prayer, I strolled behind the boys onto the football field where I watched the entire game on the sidelines, barely conversing during the competition.

When the football team played their games away, I rode on the bus with coaches and students. I sometimes sat in the front by Larry Fitzgerald, Jr., the star running back, who after competing at Holy Angels and the University of Pittsburgh, went on to become a professional football player for the Arizona Cardinals. We spoke from time to time while on the bus.

I always respected Larry not only on the football field, but also in class, on the rare times I taught religion. He was thoughtful, humble, and genuinely attentive in the class, with reverence for his peers. Not surprisingly, he carried with him these qualities onto the field.

Having settled into both parishes and at the academy by early fall, I was keen on renovating the main floor of Saint Boniface's rectory. The first stage, before starting the remodeling and after receiving at least two estimates, was to receive consent by the two lay parish trustees and then obtain authorization, by proxy, from the Spiritual Leader of the Archdiocese and Vicar General, the right-hand man of the Archbishop. This was due to the project's cost, anticipated to be over $25,000. The expected cost projected was about $100,000.00.

Each parish within the Archdiocese of Saint Paul and Minneapolis is a single corporation with five board members which include the archbishop, vicar general, pastor, and two lay parish trustees. The trustees, who are parishioners of that parish, customarily are well connected to the parish as well as savvy on business affairs. They serve for two years, which can be renewed as often as all parties concur to it.

In late September, with everything in order and approved, the renovations began. The smoked-filled carpet in five rooms and the twelve-foot-wide hall were removed first. The bathroom attached to the former pastor's bedroom was completely gutted and was to become the storage closet; his sleeping quarters became my main office.

All five rooms received a fresh coat of paint. One room that in the past was used as a community room was painted a blood red color and was called the "Red Room." In addition to this room's wood flooring being stripped and polished, the floors of my main office and the adjoining sitting room by the entrance parlor where I saw, or counseled parishioners were redone. To harmonize with the already built-in bookshelves in the sitting room, I had more con-structed for the east wall of my main office.

A major makeover took place in the kitchen, which had black-ened walls and a moderately sized pantry. The original intention for the kitchen included new appliances, custom-crafted cabinets, and new flooring. Two south windows located in the pantry, which were covered up with painted sheetrock, were to be restored. A father and his son who were hired to begin all the work, with the excep-tion of laying down the new granite flooring, arrived on a Monday. During the first week the cabinets were removed. On Friday the father-son team left for the weekend.

Apart from hearing Confessions and celebrating two Masses each weekend, the majority of my time was used to pursue my hobby of reading and continue my drinking habit. That particular weekend, when all the cabinets were gone, I was determined to make an alteration in the prearranged blueprint of the kitchen and pantry. Late Friday night, drunk, I picked up a hammer and started to knock out the wall between the kitchen and pantry, since I now desired a countertop with a sit-down bar on the pantry side.

My hazardous destruction of the wall running with electrical wires between the studs took several hours and ended in the morning. The floor, now a dangerous mess from all the sheetrock and nails, would be cleaned up the next night, again while I was plastered.

On Monday morning, father and son entered the kitchen to start nailing the newly constructed cabinets to the walls, their faces divulging intense unhappiness in what had occurred over the weekend. Needless to say, the father expressed his disapproval of my doings, originally not designed for the kitchen and pantry. My conduct produced not only a momentous disagreement but also hard feelings between the father and me, which I would not realize were caused by the severity of my drunken actions until years later.

Remarkably the remodeling was completed in a relatively short time. Although ashamed by my behavior that weekend, the kitchen and pantry turned out to be an exquisite room, practical and well-designed, one I relished cooking in for the remainder of my assignment at the parish.

During this time, my drinking increased with each succeeding year. At this point, my consuming of alcohol was either a bottle of gin or vodka in one week. My hangovers became more regular, although I did not believe it affected my work. Endeavors to stop for a few days at a time were more or less successful, thus convincing myself I was not consuming an unhealthy amount of alcohol and better yet, I was not an alcoholic.

In the first months of my threefold appointment, I traveled two long-distance flights—one to Hawaii and the other to Rome. The trip to Hawaii was a week-long retreat in Honolulu which was held at a church that was staffed by the Oratory of Saint Philip Neri Community. This unique religious community was comprised of priests and lay-brothers that live together united by no formal vows, but simply with the oath of charity. The retreat was non-directed, allowing me to have frequent periods of prayer and time for reflection, reading, and writing.

Following my time on Oahu, I then flew to Maui for another week. My friend Bob, who had left his priesthood formation from the St. Paul Seminary after our second year was completed, was now getting married. Bob, with his fiancée Naoko, whom I'd never met, picked me up at the airport. We drove back admiring the lush tropical view and catching up on old times. Once at the resort, all three of us sat outside discussing their wedding ceremony that I would help celebrate in the next few days at a Catholic church. It felt good to be asked to preside at his and Naoko's nuptial observance. Once again, Bob's inclusion of me on the most important day of his life generated a rare sense of importance within me; I always longed to be included.

I stayed in Bob's parents' room sleeping in the loft. Of the twenty-one guests invited to the wedding, I was the only non–family member. The time spent with Bob and his family at the matrimony service and during the week was relaxing. In addition to the wedding day, Bob's sister Katie, her husband Arnie, and I drove up to the peak of Haleakalā volcano. The deep hues of green coating the mountainside and the majestic surroundings allowed me time to ponder the greatness of God's work.

Two months following my journey to Hawaii, I flew in the opposite direction, this time to Rome. My good friend Agnes and her daughter, Mary Ann, accompanied me to the Eternal City. Mary Ann's son was studying abroad for the semester, and this trip gave mother and son some time to catch up. We rented rooms at a convent whose community members have dwindled over the years.

Unfortunately, this is not an uncommon occurrence for the majority of religious organizations these days, and this brought about numerous empty rooms, now made available for tourists and pilgrims.

Besides exploring Vatican City and other churches, I celebrated Mass at one of the side chapels at the Saint Paul Basilica outside the walls of Rome. In addition to seeing that church, we stopped by at the Saint John Lateran Basilica, the mother church of the Archdiocese of Rome, where the Bishop of the diocese is the Pope.

While in Honolulu, I dropped into a Catholic bookstore and began searching for a book to read. I discovered one that captivated my interest after scanning the back cover. The book was about the life of Saint Gabriel Possenti, whom I knew nothing about. I read the book while on my retreat in Hawaii and learned about this holy man. Saint Gabriel of Our Lady of Sorrows lived during the middle of the nineteenth century, became a professed religious Passionist brother, and succumbed to tuberculosis at the age of twenty-three. After quickly reading the book, I yearned to one day visit his shrine in Isola del Gran Sasso in Italy. Now that I was in Italy, the opportunity had presented itself.

My pilgrimage to Isola del Gran Sasso began at six in the morning. Initially I walked to the subway station, then to a bus station, hoping that it would take me to Teramo, which was where I needed to go. When I saw a sign, "Teramo Bus Station," inscribed only in Italian, I concluded by the symbol and seeing other buses parked in the area that this was my spot to step off the bus. With hunger pangs grasping at my stomach, I searched for food, finding some fruit at a nearby roadside stand to consume.

I struggled to flag down a taxi, and was unproductive at my first several efforts, but finally a driver, although he spoke no English, realized that I sought to go to Saint Gabriel's shrine. At last, following a brief ride, my dream of seeing the place had been accomplished. As I approached the entry to where Saint Gabriel's body lay inside a glass tomb, a notice attached to the door noted the shrine would be closed from noon until four, which is typical in Italy. It was currently 11:40 a.m., which permitted me just twenty minutes to pray in front of this holy man's tomb—a Catholic tradition—and a quick stop at the bookstore.

While in the bookstore, among the items I procured was a sixteen-inch-high statue of Saint Gabriel that I hand-carried all the way back to Minnesota. Because the shrine would close soon, very few people were present. I strolled over to the only café nearby to ask about getting a taxi back to Teramo; no one spoke a word of English. Thus, I walked back to the shrine where an enormous monument stood of Saint Gabriel at the entrance to the parking lot. No cars, no people, no traffic were to be spotted for the longest stretch.

I stood in front of the statue, looked up, and desperately shouted out loud, "Saint Gabriel of Our Lady of Sorrows, please get me back to Rome." Within two minutes, an empty bus came around the corner and stopped; the driver opened his window and with a little English asked where I wanted to travel to. I told him, "Teramo."

He responded, "Get on," in English.

When we entered the Teramo bus station, with broken English, he inquired about my next destination.

"Rome," I replied.

The driver directed me to the location for the bus heading to Rome. I purchased my ticket and off I was to Rome. Twelve and a half hours later, famished and with a throbbing headache, I reached the convent, thankful to Saint Gabriel for interceding on my behalf and getting me back to Rome.

Throughout the first months of 2001, my life at the parishes and at the high school was fairly uneventful. During the summer, my friend Doug lived in one of the rectory rooms as he aided me in attempting to increase Saint Boniface's population, landscaping around the parish grounds, and editing my weekly bulletin articles. One of the highlights of Doug's labors was constructing a garden bed on the southeast side of the rectory ground's rich soil since it was only a few blocks from the Mississippi River.

Across the parking lot on the same block stood Saint Maron Maronite Catholic Church—an Eastern rite church in union with the Pope. At the time, I was not aware of the fact that within the Catholic Church there are twenty-three Eastern Rite Churches and one Western Rite, universally identified as the Roman Catholic Church, the most populous one. The principal differences between the different rites are their geographical origin, different ways of celebrating the Eucharist, as well as how they name things. For instance, in the Roman Catholic tradition there are "dioceses," while in the Eastern rite the term "eparchy" is used.

Father or Abouna sharbel, pastor of Saint Maron, introduced himself immediately after I came to northeast Minneapolis. They were preparing to erect a new worship area and add office spaces. He asked me, during the construction period, if they could utilize our church to worship. I agreed. During this time, not only did I become familiar with the Maronite Rite, but also, I got to know their parishioners. My relationship with Abouna sharbel and the Maronites grew during my years at Saint Boniface and continued to flourish in the years to come.

CHAPTER 14

Reflections and Loss

U nlike prior years in my threefold assignments, the end of the year 2001 developed into an exceptionally historic one, both individually and universally. A ten-day pilgrimage to Guatemala and El Salvador was the first event of this unique year. I participated in the Maryknoll Fathers and Brothers–sponsored journey during February along with nineteen other priests from around the United States.

I landed in Guatemala City, which would serve as our home base while touring the country. We learned about the people, culture, and civil war where numerous individuals were killed including the martyrdom of Father Stanley Rother, a Catholic priest from the Archdiocese of Oklahoma City serving in the parish of Santiago Atitlan along the shores of Central America's deepest waters—Lake Atitlán. We stopped at the nearby parish of San Lucas Toliman, whose pastor was Father Gregory Shaffer, an uncle of one of my seminary classmates, who had ministered and supported the local population for over forty years.

My favorite component of this pilgrimage was traveling around El Salvador. We saw many places where Catholic priests and laypersons were martyred during the civil war within the country. First, we went to see the road on which Rutilio Grande, a Jesuit, along with two parishioners in 1977 were shot and killed as they drove. Then, we stopped at the site where four Catholic churchwomen were raped and killed on December 2, 1980. Next, we stopped on the grounds of the University of Central America (USC) to view the memorial of six Jesuit priests, along with a mother and her daughter, who were gunned down in 1989.

At the height of El Salvador's civil war, Saint Archbishop Oscar Romero was martyred as he celebrated Mass at a hospital chapel. The most poignant aspect of this pilgrimage arose when we celebrated Mass at the altar where Romero died. Following Mass, we prayed at his tomb, lying below in the San Salvador's cathedral crypt. This journey not only increased my faith, but also triggered me to become more actively involved in social justice concerns, particularly in Central America.

The second major event in 2001 transpired on May 13— Mother's Day that year. At 5:30 in the morning, my mom telephoned to let me know that my brother Christopher had died at the age of thirty-one—an early death due to his lifelong poor health conditions and disability. Even though Chris' death was expected, as he had been declining in those recent weeks, it nonetheless was startling. Two days later, I flew to Grand Junction, Colorado, where I officiated at his funeral Mass. Presiding at my brother's funeral was emotional for me. As I delivered the homily, I felt tears building up; thus, I asked Chris to help me get through his service. It worked! I was then able to hold my emotions intact.

The following day, Mom and I, transporting his cremains, drove to Kansas for a second funeral service at Saint Joseph's Church in Scott City, the place of his baptism. His burial took place in a local cemetery next to his dad. Finally, after thirty-one years of a difficult life, Chris now rested in peace.

To be honest—sometimes this is challenging for me to do— Christopher's death created both sadness and relief. Sadness I had lost my brother, and relief feeling now we could have a break from having to take care of someone. Soon after his death, my sisters presented my mom with a puppy. I believe this helped her with her grief tremendously, as she received unconditional love and was able to continue to nurture now that she no longer had Christopher. Of course, I know she had no intention, yet at times I felt less important in her life as this puppy was another thing to take her attention from me.

Six weeks after Chris' funeral service, I flew west to Los Altos, located between San Jose and San Francisco, for a thirty-day retreat at the Jesuit Retreat Center. The retreat was a form of the Spiritual Exercises of Saint Ignatius of Loyola. Originally meant for the Jesuits, presently any individual, rather than a priest, brother, or layperson, may involve themselves in this way of prayer for one month for any number of purposes: to make a major decision in life, during a time of renewal or on sabbatical, as part of one's spiritual direction training, or in my circumstances, to deepen my spiritual life.

To prepare us for the thirty-day silent retreat, we were instructed for two days about what to expect from it as well as how we might receive the maximum amount of fruits from this form of prayer. We were asked to maintain silence at all times, even during our meals. Assigned to each participant was a spiritual director who was derived from a number of priests or nuns, and whom we would visit with once a day. I hoped for a priest, but instead, for my spiritual director, a Presentation sister was assigned to me.

When the retreat began, in addition to daily direction, we were required to take four or five one-hour periods throughout the day and early evening for prayer. In virtually all prayer times, I sat or kneeled in the chapel. At first, I found it challenging to pray for an hour at a time; however, midway through the thirty days, the hour of prayer typically flew by. Once a day we all gathered for the celebration of Mass.

Since sustaining silence was not any trouble for me, I appreciated all the quiet moments, except during meals. We were not permitted to use hand gestures either, unless requesting the salt or pepper.

The distinctiveness of Spiritual Exercises lay in Saint Ignatius' utilizing of one's imagination while meditating on the scriptures, especially on the Gospels. You were to enter into the scene of a biblical passage as if you yourself were there. This powerful technique that I acquired would aid me to help formulate a correct decision, whether minor or major. After making a choice, Saint Ignatius would have one reflect upon it and then see how you felt a brief time later. If one was at peace and not irritable, you had reached a true choice; if one was restless and irritable the right choice was not reached. Eighteen years later, I still find this exercise extremely valuable in my decision making.

At the end of the thirty days, we were provided one more day to ease back towards our lives in the outside world. On the last night, a banquet was served to celebrate our success.

Before I came to Los Altos, I intentionally desired to break from my alcohol addiction. Therefore, I deliberately abstained from liquor throughout the period even though I could have strolled to a nearby store. Since I thought I simply had a drinking problem but was not an alcoholic, I was convinced that my triumph after thirty nondrinking days proved my point.

Wrong! The moment I was back in Minnesota, my consuming of alcohol picked up right where it had been left off.

Six weeks later on September 8, I drove to Jordan, Minnesota, where a friend, Father John, pastored Saint John the Baptist Parish. After a pleasant evening, around 11 p.m., I returned to Minneapolis. Driving along Highway 169, I reflected on the peaceful, restful, smooth ride home. Perhaps this Friday evening experience of calmness I enjoyed would be enough to sustain me following the tragic aftermath our nation would soon encounter, three days later.

The following Tuesday was sunny and warm. Before walking to my office after Mass, I strolled around behind the church to observe how the repairs were coming on the parking lot above the boiler room that was beginning to deteriorate. Once completing the inspection, satisfied, I proceeded to my office, but not before stopping to say hello to the secretary.

"Did you hear?" she quizzed.

"Hear what?" I answered back.

"The attack on the World Trade Center in New York City," my secretary replied.

"No," I responded with disbelief, and then informed her, "I will go up and turn on the television."

Without delay, I walked to my sitting room, saw what was transpiring, and continued to watch the news coverage throughout the day until evening, when a pastoral council meeting had been scheduled. The parishioners on the council and I gathered; yet, instead of calling to order the meeting, the whole evening was taken up by our chatting about that catastrophic day.

Earlier that May, I left my chaplaincy position at Academy of Holy Angels. Furthermore, since Saints Cyril and Methodius Church was now under the guidance of an Ecuadorian pastor, and no longer my responsibility, my assignment now only encompassed Saint Boniface. The parish of less than two hundred souls to minister to demanded little, if any, of my time, triggering an increase in my boredom. Therefore, I requested an uncommon transfer—that is, to offer my priestly ministry outside the Archdiocese.

The average Catholic parishioner is unaccustomed to the procedure for how and where a diocesan or secular priest can be transferred by his bishop. Unlike in the religious orders, where a superior can assign one of his priests anywhere around the world, provided the local bishop sanctions it, a secular priest is ordinarily relocated by his bishop within the geographic area of his diocese. When a diocesan priest, such as myself, asks for an appointment to a parish or Catholic institution outside of his diocese, he must receive both the consent from his bishop and then obtain permission from the bishop whose diocese he wants to be transferred to.

I worked through this course of action, as I sought to be appointed somewhere within the Archdiocese of Denver. Imagining I could visit and be closer to my family, this seemed to ease a fear inside of me, knowing once again I would not be so alone. Flying out to Colorado in August, I met with Archbishop Chaput and his vicar general. My meetings were beneficial; I was invited to come to their Archdiocese, soon thereafter serving as a parochial vicar or an assistant pastor. I also learned that my appointment would not be discerned until January, this since my intentions were to move during that month.

CHAPTER 15

A Year of Change

Archbishop Chaput's letter of appointment appeared in the mailbox the second week of 2002. He was assigning me, effective February 1, to Notre Dame Church located on the southwest corner of Denver. I would be serving as the second associate pastor to Monsignor Leo. Father Walter, a priest in his eighties originally from Switzerland, was his first parochial vicar.

After reading the letter, I immediately investigated Notre Dame Church's website and discovered it furnished little information about the parish. Later that day, I telephoned Leo to inquire about his parish, and when I could move in since my last day at Saint Boniface would be in the middle of January. He decided my arrival would be the last week in January.

Since the present second associate occupied what was to become my living quarters, I would stay in the guest room until he left. Even though it was my desire to commence my ministry right away, the traditional, Pre-Vatican yet holy pastor would not allow it until the date of the official appointment. I was beginning to doubt my judgement in asking for the transfer to Denver.

One week later, I emptied the boxes and suitcases containing some of my belongings and decided to leave the majority of my possessions in storage in my friend Agnes' basement. While my bedroom was located on the second floor, my office was in the basement surrounded by additional workspaces for the staff.

The preschool and elementary school building was two blocks

from the church. The sacred building could accommodate six hundred souls and had been recently remodeled. I found the worship area a tranquil space for prayer, particularly the tiny side chapel with the tabernacle holding the Blessed Sacrament. I celebrated my first Mass at Notre Dame on February 1. The parishioners were gracious and welcoming.

With three priests in the parish, Monsignor Leo treated Walter and me with respect, but his authority was palpable. I was given no choice about which day I could have off as Leo notified me that it would be Monday. He further told me he had assigned every Tuesday and Friday to me as "duty days." I'd presumed the term "duty days" no longer existed, but not at Notre Dame. "Duty days" was a term dating from the pre-Vatican era, before 1965. These were days that one of the priests in the parish would be on call, allocating any walk-ins, hospital emergencies, death or sick calls to him. This entailed that I remain at the rectory throughout the day. One time I left for 15 minutes to go four blocks to a grocery store, and during my brief absence a sick call arose. Needless to say, Leo was not at all happy with me. From this point forward, for the rest of my time at Notre Dame, I either kept my cell phone with me or lingered at the rectory the entire day. I had learned my lesson!

The responsibilities delegated above and beyond duty days included Baptisms performed about once every six weeks, limited marriage preparations, weddings, and visits to Notre Dame's school. If a parishioner died on one of my duty days, then I officiated at his or her funeral Mass. Whenever my schedule would allow, I chose to join the youth of the parish for their weekly gathering.

At my first funeral at Notre Dame, I instantly realized what I had been taught in the seminary and how things were done very differently here. Fr. Leo had a way of presiding, positioning the flowers and plants, and placing the location of the Easter candle which I had never seen. I performed these tasks the way I had been taught by Father Mike at Saint Pius X. According to Leo, this was not the correct placement. After yelling at me, he would proceed to move things to their "proper" location. Switching my status after three and a half years as my own boss back to an associate pastor sure had its challenges some days.

In spite of the disagreement with Leo, I came to realize that there could be other styles used to accomplish the same tasks, and all of them were correct. By the time I left Notre Dame, I genuinely valued seeing beyond one way of undertaking certain ideas, which would be tremendously advantageous in my future ministry at other parishes. I am grateful to have served under two relatively contrasting pastors, both of whom taught me important lessons in my priestly ministry.

Since the thirty-day retreat where I refrained successfully from alcohol, six months after arriving in Denver, once again I sought to control my drinking. I purchased no alcohol and there was none in the rectory—so I thought. I managed to abstain from drinking for one month. This triumph would be my last for over a decade.

One night at Notre Dame as I searched for toilet paper in a storage closet, I came across a full bottle of vodka. Even though I didn't want to drink, my dependence on alcohol was too strong. I carried the vodka bottle to my room, went downstairs to find some orange juice, grabbed a tumbler, returned to my sitting room, mixed the two liquids together, and guzzled it down. I had two more drinks. After I finished, I put the bottle back in the closet. One week later, I noticed the vodka had not been touched, so I made myself more drinks. Again, four days later, I went back to the closet. When I emptied the bottle after five drinking episodes,

I drove to the closest liquor store, purchased more alcohol, and returned to the rectory. I made myself several more drinks, which I downed over the evening hours until falling asleep. I continued this behavior for several more months and moved on to heavier drinking as my tolerance to alcohol intensified. By early fall that year, my nightly drinking began in late afternoon and continued throughout the night.

I experienced few repercussions in the morning—or so I believed. Because my nightly routine occurred alone in my room, Leo, Walter, or anyone else knew nothing about my addiction, or if they did, they held it to themselves. I was secretive about bringing alcohol home, and either put the bottle in a larger grocery bag or waited until evening when I was confident that I would not run into someone.

At this point, I'd established a buying schedule. Since I purchased liquor every four or five days, I would patronize a store every sixth time in order not to become known by employees. These numerous stores were convenient as they were all located within three miles of the rectory. This became my routine for the duration of my stay in Colorado.

Six months into my Notre Dame post, I received a telephone call from the pastor at the local Maronite Catholic Mission called Saint Rafka. Abouna Jacob invited me out for dinner. While at the restaurant, he mentioned that he had heard I knew about their ritual from Abouna sharbel back in Minneapolis. He asked if I would celebrate Mass for him at the Mission since he was going back home to Lebanon for an unknown period. Jacob pointed out that I could say the Mass in the Latin Rite as his parishioners had been acclimated to this not too long ago. I agreed.

Saint Rafka was a newly erected mission of the Eparchy of

Our Lady of Lebanon with Jacob as its first full-time pastor. At the time, All Souls Roman Catholic Church provided the mission with a house, rent-free. I was to celebrate their Divine Liturgy in the worship space late Sunday afternoons. The original Mass I presided over for the Maronite Catholic community was on the Assumption of the Blessed Virgin Mary. The following Sunday through the end of September, I celebrated the Latin Rite Mass each week. Since the Masses scheduled at Saint Rafka never interfered with my obligations at Notre Dame, Leo supported my additional ministry. Moreover, I anticipated ending my service once Jacob came back in the fall.

As the date neared to when we thought he would be back, Jacob, however, did not return to Englewood. I discovered through a parishioner that his absence was extended for another month. Consequently, my services were sought once again, and I accepted the invitation. Once that month ended, there was still no sign that Jacob would be returning any time soon.

Hence my Sunday afternoons continued at Saint Rafka celebrating Mass. As the months came and went, it became obvious that Jacob would not be returning at all. The mission community, with the permission of the bishop and vicar general of the Eparchy, requested that I stay on until a replacement was appointed. All the while, I was struggling more and more at Notre Dame.

Guessing my intentions, Father Gregory, the Eparchy's vicar general, persuaded me to delay returning to the Archdiocese of Saint Paul and Minneapolis for an additional year in order that I might be appointed the parochial administrator of Saint Rafka. Of course, I needed my Archbishop's permission to do this, and he gave his permission.

Although All Souls Church allowed us the use of one of their houses that included a bedroom which previously Jacob had had, I preferred to live in residence at another church. A newly appointed priest named Michael asked if I wanted to live in his rectory at Saint Aelred of Rievaulx Parish in the northern area of Denver. I accepted his offer and moved in at the end of June.

Six days a week, I drove to Saint Rafka, occasionally sleeping over if there was a late-night meeting. As the months passed, I began to spend most of my time at the house on Pennwood Circle. It was small in size, but I liked the quiet neighborhood and the simplicity of the dwelling.

My addiction to alcohol continued while I served at Saint Rafka, except for the fact that I didn't feel the need to completely hide it. I always had one bottle hidden in my bedroom closet. A couple other bottles I left in a kitchen cabinet so that I could offer a cocktail to any visitors.

Knowing that I would eventually return to Minnesota after my year at Saint Rafka, in February I flew to Minnesota to meet with Father Samuel, who still remained the Director of the Priests' Personnel Board. A list containing fifteen parishes whose pastors were leaving their parishes was presented to me. Two or three parishes interested me, one of which was in south Minneapolis. The following Sunday I attended Mass at the parish in Minneapolis and visited with the pastor, who gave a tour of the church, offices, and school. While I thought I would be considered for this parish, Samuel suggested another parish called Saint Gregory the Great in North Branch, forty-five miles north of Saint Paul.

Since I was not acquainted with this parish, I shared with Samuel my lack of interest in being assigned there. Nonetheless, he insisted that I consider it, extending no other hints that I should explore other parishes on the list. Still not drawn to Saint Gregory the Great, I exited his office with no clear notion of which parish I might be assigned to that coming July.

By May 1st, I was no further along in determining which parish to apply to. I contacted Father Samuel, who once again continued to propose Saint Gregory the Great Parish and no other.

At that point, I decided that I might as well look into the parish. I flew to Minnesota, drove up to North Branch in order to tour and be introduced to the staff of Saint Gregory the Great. I was still not interested in going to this parish since this was not only a small parish, but also more crucially, it was essentially a rural parish in a bedroom community. My lack of desire to go to this parish had nothing to do with the parishioners. I simply wished to serve a parish in either Saint Paul, Minneapolis, or a neighboring suburb.

Bishop Pates, the auxiliary bishop in the Archdiocese, called on my cell phone one day late in May to advise me that Archbishop Flynn wanted to appoint me to Saint Gregory the Great Parish. Bishop Pates was requesting that I say "yes." Feeling that I had no choice again, I accepted the assignment.

In the intervening time, one of my chief accomplishments while at Saint Rafka was changing this mission church into a non-profit entity in the State of Colorado with its own legal name. This necessitated that I go to an auxiliary building of the State Capitol to apply and obtain a tax ID number and formalize the church's bank accounts. I always wanted to be a founding pastor of some parish, so now, to a certain extent, at least on the business side of the mission, I had. Moreover, I received satisfaction knowing that in the history of Saint Rafka Mission, I played an important role in this community's establishment. Again, my gift of organizational skills was realized during my assignment at this church.

Once Saint Rafka was developed into a legal cooperation, my

remaining time in Denver was spent searching for a place that we could call our permanent home. Funding would need to be raised and a location chosen. The decision as to whether we should buy land and construct a church or purchase an existing building that could be converted into a Maronite Catholic Church had to be made. Father Gregory flew to Denver one weekend to assist some men from the parish in our pursuit of a new home. After he was appointed as bishop for another eparchy, the new vicar general, Father Isaiah, traveled to Denver in the spring to meet for dinner with several members of our community and myself.

Before going to the restaurant, I drank two cocktails. While at the restaurant I had two glasses of wine. While waiting for our meal to be served, I became upset with how the discussion between the vicar general and parishioners began. Having too much alcohol clouding my thinking and becoming more upset with how the conversation was going, I stormed out of the restaurant without saying a word.

I had attempted to interject my thoughts into the conversation that night; however, I felt dismissed and my words appeared to be ignored. The prior vicar general, who I was more familiar with, seemed more gentle, always listening to what I had to say. I was more comfortable with his way of handling things. Now, I was having a struggle getting used to the new vicar general's way of doing things.

Not a single person from that night uttered a word to me. Not only did I feel ashamed of my behavior, but I also questioned why no one said anything to me about my unprofessional actions. Another piece of assurance that I most certainly was not an alcoholic, as it did not seem to bother anyone. Throughout the ensuing years, very few individuals ever mentioned to me that they recognized my drinking habit or were alarmed by it, allowing me to repeatedly tell myself I did not have a problem.

By the end of my appointment at Saint Rafka, although the community was not ready to acquire land or an existing church building, they were in an excellent position to do so when my successor came the following August. Father Armando arrived at the mission church a month before I left Englewood for Minnesota, in order that there might be a smooth changeover of spiritual leadership.

On a late August day, I journeyed to Minnesota for a few days before heading to Bellarmine Jesuit Retreat House in Barrington, a suburb of Chicago. Just before traveling off to Illinois, I received a distressing e-mail from my friend Bob, now living in Japan. He wrote disclosing he had one month to live. He had cancer. Bob wished that I could come to Osaka for one final visit, but he understood that it would probably be unlikely since I was in the middle of a transition between parishes.

After debating whether or not I should fly to Japan for a day, I definitely felt like I needed to see Bob one more time; thus, I made reservations to fly to Osaka once my retreat was completed. When my long-distance flight arrived, somehow I successfully, without speaking any Japanese, found the right bus to take me to the hospital that Bob was in. Late in the evening, I entered Bob's room to say hello to my dear friend. Since he was quite exhausted, I stayed only a passing moment before leaving with his parents Bill and Nancy to our hotel.

Besides Bob's parents, two of his sisters likewise were in Japan to see their brother. He had become too weak to talk, although he could write to communicate with everyone. Bob wished to celebrate Mass one last time on Sunday, which I was able to provide, giving him what would be his final opportunity to receive Holy Communion.

On the fifth day, I cried my good-byes before heading back to

Minnesota, realizing that I would never see him again. To this day, I continue to have teary eyes when I think about Bob's all-too-brief life. Bob was one of the few people who accepted me as I am—a true friend.

A New Place to Call Home

Following a ten-hour layover in Honolulu, my Northwest Airline flight landed at the Minneapolis and Saint Paul International Airport about 6:20 on the morning of September 14, 2004, the day I began as pastor of Saint Gregory the Great in North Branch. I arrived at my elderly friend Agnes' home, where I stayed for two weeks until some work was completed at the rectory. Before going to my new parish, I took a lengthy nap. When I arrived at the parish, I began rearranging and organizing my new office while meeting with some parishioners and the staff.

As 6:00 p.m. approached, I prepared to celebrate my first Mass at the parish at the regularly scheduled Tuesday night service. Bishop Pates had allowed me to choose the date to start my appointment, so I selected that day since it was the Feast of the Triumph of the Holy Cross—one of my favorite feast days in the Catholic Church. I was informed that six to ten parishioners usually showed up at this evening Mass. That night, 65 individuals came to see their new pastor and to welcome me! As soon as Mass was finished and all the parishioners had gone home, I drove back to White Bear Lake for the night.

The following Sunday, a parishioner requested that I allow him to speak before all the Masses in order to motivate others to support and participate in our annual Booya and Fall Festival the next weekend. Until that Sunday, I had never heard of a "Booya," which I soon learned was a fall tradition in the Upper Midwest when stew was cooked outdoors in giant kettles overnight. With this event, I anticipated a great opportunity to meet many of my new parishioners. This did happen as I greeted parishioners while they stood in the line waiting to get their stew!

My first Booya day was overshadowed by an early morning telephone call. Nancy, Bob's mom, called to tell me Bob had died. I remember lying on my bed grieving the loss of my close friend just as if it happened yesterday. I presided at his funeral memorial services a few weeks later—an extremely emotional and tough one for me.

A month after returning to Minnesota, I needed to schedule my annual physical. Since my current physician had just retired, I contacted another doctor recommended to me in Minneapolis, Dr. Mary McMillan, to see if she was taking any new patients. She was, so I scheduled an appointment for the end of October.

During this time, I continued drinking, primarily at night after my meetings would be finished. I recognized I definitely had a problem but continued to deny being an alcoholic. I was still determined to get control over my dependence on alcohol. When the scheduled time to see my new doctor came, I handed her three handwritten pages regarding the history of my consumption of liquor. For the first time I was candid about my encounters with alcohol, apart from convincing myself that I wasn't an alcoholic. Naturally, Dr. McMillan firmly encouraged me to decrease my drinking of vodka or any other spirits. I agreed to her suggestion.

Within a few weeks of this appointment, as is predictable of a full-fledged alcoholic, my behavior returned to its previous routine. Even worse, I now began to finish off a bottle of vodka almost every three days. One of the fundamental excuses for believing that I was not an alcoholic was that even if I had a hangover, I could still work through the day without having any blackouts, and the drinking did not interfere with my relationships. Not that I had many close relationships. All of my drinking took place in the privacy of the rectory when I was alone.

As time stretched on, I started drinking earlier and earlier in the day. The combination of the lack of work, few relationships, fear of not being liked or accepted, as well as being bored stiff fueled my drinking. From the very beginning, I had considered my assignment to Saint Gregory the Great an incomplete application of my gifts and time. Not only that, I was in a town away from the Twin Cities where a large number of my parishioners commuted into the Cities to work, thus leaving them exhausted and having little energy to participate in either evening or weekend activities. Despite this, the parish did have a passable number of dedicated parishioners who volunteered their time and talents.

While possessing a strong German work ethic, I needed to stay busy with church work and not have to continuously look for things to occupy my time. Likewise, having a talented and outstanding administrative assistant (who held the position for over twenty years) to manage the business affairs of the parish, left me with even fewer responsibilities apart from having final voice on important matters. On the pastoral side, Deacon Tom and his wife Elizabeth, who lived next door in a house owned by Saint Gregory the Great, provided the parish with many of its pastoral needs. We were overstaffed at that time.

My introversion and lack of self-confidence once again became a problem for me at my new parish. Whenever I had to meet with a parishioner for any matter, such as preparing for a funeral Mass or counseling, I always kept these appointments brief. My fearfulness of others caused parishioners to think I was insensitive and unapproachable. Many felt I didn't care about them or their concerns.

Looking back at my life, I now realize another cause of my addiction was the absence of meaningful and life-giving relationships and friendships with my family or with others. This reality created further isolation in addition to being physically distant from family, friends, and my brother priests. I never understood why my immediate or extended family never communicated or worked on developing relationships with each other. During my life, it has always been I who made phone calls or went to see family members. Likewise, it seems I have always been the one to initiate and maintain friendships outside of my family as well. I do not put any criticism on family or friends, since these relationships (or lack of them) have been generated by my being timid and by my former inability to express my feelings and needs.

The impact of alcoholism became more profound in late 2005. Now I was waking up in the middle of the night unable to go back to sleep for hours, experiencing bouts of depression, having frequent episodes of vomiting in the mornings, and feeling miserable during the day. For the first time, thoughts of suicide entered my head. Two days after Christmas that year, my depression and suicidal thoughts became so powerful that I contacted a doctor in North Branch, who asked to see me right away.

The physician who walked in the examination room was an older gentleman who told me he was quite knowledgeable about the lives of Catholic priests. He shared stories about his time on the Iron Range of northern Minnesota and his association with ministers of all faiths while serving in the area. He understood the loneliness and monotony which often occurs with clergy of diverse religious backgrounds, and their experiences living and ministering in small towns with little or no support system, particularly Catholic priests, who by a manmade law, were obligated to be celibate.

After we finished our discussion, he suggested that I have someone take me to the Cambridge Medical Center for observation. He stepped out of the room for a minute to place a call and find out if the hospital had a room available. He soon returned and instructed me to have someone immediately drive me the fifteen miles to the city of Cambridge, as he did not want me to travel alone.

Once back at the rectory, I contacted Deacon Tom at St. Gregory the Great, asking him to come over right away. I wanted to explain to him in person my suicidal thoughts and the situation I was now in. After a short discussion, he agreed to give me a ride to the medical center. In a few moments, we were on our way with my small bag carrying a change of clothing and some toiletries.

Together we entered the hospital and walked up to the admissions desk. When they asked why I was here, I was directed to the psychiatric ward. My heart sunk. I had not realized that my doctor was sending me to this area in the medical center. I was scared, and not so convinced I wanted to stay. I was told the hospital would hold me for seventy-two hours unless something changed their mind or if they believed that I was no longer in jeopardy of harming myself. Then Deacon Tom embraced me and said, "I am here for you if you need anything."

After guiding me to the room I would be sharing with one other patient and explaining the policies of the psychiatric area, my vitals were taken, and blood work was drawn. The nurse directed me to a large room where other patients were there for the same purpose. I felt out of place and chose to sit alone at a table away from all activity. When the time arrived for a cigarette break, every single patient strolled outside into a confined space except for me.

The staff later apprised us to get ready for bed and that lights out would occur in ten minutes. My roommate and I scarcely spoke to each other. I had been taking a prescription sleeping pill and it was not with me, so along with withdrawing from alcohol, I found it impossible to fall asleep. I tossed and turned throughout the night. The light from the hall would brighten the room as the staff checked on us on the hour. Still incapable of falling asleep, around four o'clock in the morning, I walked to the nurse station, requesting that since I had not brought with me a sleeping pill they give me a substitute. They refused. All they would offer me was a cup of hot tea to see if that would help. It did not. Eventually, I did fall asleep about an hour later.

In the morning I ate only one piece of bread, given that I was feeling queasy. Later that day, a female alcohol counselor spoke with me. I was not entirely truthful when disclosing my information to her; however, I was honest enough during my evaluation for her to understand I was in fact an alcoholic. The counselor fervently recommended that I participate in an inpatient treatment program as soon as possible. I refused and told her I would be consulting my doctor to develop a strategy to limit my drinking as well as seeing a new therapist.

Completing my evaluation and realizing I was no longer a threat to my life, they released me from the hospital. Deacon Tom came to get me. I returned home, concealing all that had happened to me over the past twenty-four hours apart from sharing only with a handful of friends and my therapist what was really happening.

The year 2006 brought routine into my world at Saint Gregory the Great. The drinking persisted as before with slight alterations. Throughout the year, I began purchasing bottles of vodka several times a month, driving nineteen miles to Forest Lake where there was a choice of liquor stores to secure my supply. The amount and frequency of alcohol I consumed, and my general health condition, remained consistent as in the prior year.

I became familiar with the parishioners' specific needs and traditions of the faith community. Since Deacon Tom was getting ready for his retirement the following year, I applied for acceptance from the Archbishop for a six-month sabbatical during the first six months of 2007. I could count on Tom to tend to the pastoral needs of the parish with the assistance of a long-term visiting priest who could celebrate Mass, hear confessions, and other sacramental needs that arose.

As long as a priest obtains agreement for his sabbatical arrangements from the Archdiocese, we are ordinarily at liberty to choose where and what we wish to accomplish during this time away. With this in mind, I opted to make an effort and achieve one of my dreams: to write and publish a book.

I desired to write in a quiet, peaceful, scenic place in a warm climate and escape Minnesota's brutal cold winter months. Because I never became a winter enthusiast, and do not enjoy activities such as snowmobiling and ice fishing, winters were grueling to endure year after year. Thus, first I contacted the Father Prior of a Benedictine priory in the Bahamas to see if he would consent to me residing in his religious community. The priest promptly wrote back apprising that the priory was closing soon since there were too few monks to keep it open, becoming a casualty of falling priestly and religious vocations in the Catholic Church.

Randomly, I searched in the *Official United States Catholic Church Book* which encompasses all the dioceses, parishes, and Catholic institutions in the country and its territories. After combing at some length through the thick book, I discovered the location where I desired to go. I sent off a letter to the vicar general of the Diocese of Saint Thomas in the US Virgin Islands, inquiring if I could occupy one of their rectories while writing my book. In exchange for my housing, I proposed my priestly ministry to occasionally celebrate Mass and other sacraments while residing there.

Two weeks later, the vicar general, William, telephoned to discuss my stay in the Virgin Islands which Bishop Murry, the diocese's bishop, had approved. The exact location of which rectory and island I would be on would not be known for a few months. Feeling good about the acceptance, I tried to remain patient wondering where exactly I would be placed.

When November arrived, I received an e-mail from William with an update informing me that I would be residing at Saints Peter and Paul Catholic Cathedral Parish on the Island of Saint Thomas where three other priests lived. One of the clerics was Father Neil. In addition to serving as the pastor at both the cathedral and its mission parish of Saint Anne, he also was the chancellor of the diocese and taught high school math at the attached K–12 school. The second priest in residence served as the principal of the school, and the third one pastored Our Lady of Perpetual Help up the hill. The rectory was in a small community, and this allowed me space to write my book and an opportunity from time to time to celebrate Mass. I was pleased with how my sabbatical arrangements effortlessly came together.

Around three o'clock in the morning on a cold January night, a parishioner dropped me off at the Minneapolis/Saint Paul airport. Besides a suitcase of all clothes, I took on the plane a heavy carry-on jammed mainly with books I hoped to read. I had previously mailed two sizeable boxes of additional books along with other items that I thought would be necessary to have during my sabbatical.

My Sun Country direct flight to Saint Thomas, half full of passengers, landed as scheduled after approximately six hours. Some travelers prepared for the heat and humidity while in flight—they had already changed into shorts and t-shirts. The minute I got off the plane, the air hit me like a rock. Beginning to sweat, I did not whine, as I was delighted to be out of the cold and snow.

Collecting my luggage, I proceeded to the passenger pick-up area, waiting for Father Neil to arrive. We quickly found each other.

I hopped into his vehicle, chatting as we headed to the cathedral rectory. Once home, he accompanied me to the room that I would be calling home for the next six months. After some lunch, I unloaded my baggage and settled into my new environment.

The two goals I desired to reach while on my sabbatical were getting control of my drinking and finishing writing a manuscript. Of course, to lessen the temptation I had not brought any liquor with me. I intended to abstain from alcohol for one whole month— something that I had not attempted in five years. For the first week, I was victorious in managing my intake. Then the following week, as I strolled down the street, I quickly discovered buying alcohol would be simpler than ever before, as spirits were sold at countless businesses. Unable to avoid the temptation, I purchased a bottle of vodka and rapidly returned to the rectory, devouring the first of what would become many drinks that day and throughout the week. Since no one ever came to my room except the cleaning lady, I did not need to agonize over someone detecting my addiction.

The same week I returned to drinking, I commenced writing my book, writing only a handful of pages due to lack of inspiration. Originally, I'd aspired to author a spiritual book, but after that week, having a daunting time being creative, I resolved to compose a novel.

At the end of the second week, Father Neil asked me, since the pastor on Saint John had left his assignment, if I would go over to the island to celebrate Masses Tuesday through Sunday. He indicated I could take the ferry back each Sunday afternoon to Saint Thomas, stay two nights at the cathedral rectory, and return every Tuesday. This request, he assured me, was for only one month until another priest could be appointed to Our Lady of Mount Carmel Parish. Furthermore, he said that I could write my book just as well as I could on Saint Thomas. I unenthusiastically agreed.

Bringing my luggage along, I rode the ferry across to Saint John

Island and then walked the short block to the rectory. My new home, located above the church offices and sacristy, was a tranquil space. I continued writing the novel on the dining-room table overlooking Cruz Bay and the Caribbean Sea. I typically composed my book late in the afternoon until just about midnight, after having two or three drinks. After writing for the day, I would have a few more. This developed into my routine for the next five and a half months of my sabbatical.

As it turned out, I would serve Our Lady of Mount Carmel throughout my time residing in the Virgin Islands, as the diocese had no priest to send for a replacement. The parishioners of the parish perceived me as their pastor, as they came to me with either questions or to render a decision on behalf of their faith community. This made for a less than desirable sabbatical as I felt I was merely shifting my duties from home to the Virgin Islands, with the exception of boundless periods for writing.

During this period, I continued my drinking and kept hidden the bottles of rum, which I now purchased, since it was inexpensive and easy to obtain in numerous shops. Before long, I learned that living in the Virgin Islands was not the location to limit or stop my liquor intake. Not a single parishioner expressed any worry about my drinking, even though I was fairly confident they were mindful of my addiction. One parishioner even came through my bedroom to repair the adjoining bathroom in which I had a bottle in plain sight that I had not had time to conceal. Nothing was said.

I completed the book the week before leaving Saint John, feeling satisfied with my accomplishment. My novel was about a young parish priest. While the main character of the book was a composite of an array of priests I knew, chapter sixteen was about a priest with a severe alcohol addiction and was the only chapter entirely about myself. I wrote the chapter while on a three-day visit to the British Virgin Islands while feeling miserable and depressed from my drinking.

Following my sabbatical, I returned to North Branch and Saint Gregory the Great, picking up where I had left off six months previously, both in drinking vodka and feeling bad physically and spiritually. My health and life was uninterrupted in its downward spiral.

CHAPTER 17

An Addition of Faith

For the next six and a half years after returning from my sabbatical, my life at St. Gregory's was essentially uneventful. There were changes in the staff at the church as I continued to fulfill my assigned pastoral duties. On July 1, 2012, I was assigned an additional parish and become pastor of Sacred Heart Parish in Rush City, the most northern parish of the Archdiocese of Saint Paul and Minneapolis.

My tolerance of alcohol continued to increase dramatically. By the middle of 2008, I now drank a bottle of liquor every two or three days. The liquor stores I frequented expanded to the surrounding cities of Stacy, Wyoming, and Cambridge, besides already going to Forest Lake. My trips to purchase vodka and at times wine never decreased since I only brought what was needed for the next two or three days.

I now started drinking in the morning on the days when I had nothing on my schedule, which was often the case. Almost no one noticed if I had been drinking, or where I was during the middle of the day. At least two or three days a week—some weeks even more—with nothing to do I would sleep off my drunkenness all afternoon.

Every so often, I attempted to stop drinking altogether. During the first day, I felt completely dreadful. I became nauseous and vomited, would sweat profusely, and was incapable of eating anything. Thoughts of suicide were relentless as were feelings of worthlessness. By the second day, I would start to feel better, and by the third day I began to feel relatively pleasant. Failing to recall just how horrible I had been feeling, I would resume my drinking on the fourth day. This pattern repeated itself many times throughout the ensuing years. Now my addiction was starting to interfere with my work, and comments were made as those around me began to notice.

Despite my dependence on alcohol, I still didn't consider myself an alcoholic. I reasoned this since I had no legal troubles, was not terminated from my employment and remained financially secure, and no relationships ended because of my drinking. If I were indeed an alcoholic, then the above would have plagued me: or so I believed.

From time to time, when comments were made by others regarding alcohol, I either laughed them off or discounted them. One afternoon, a staff member said, "Your breath smells like alcohol," then further stated, "Oh, you had Mass today," even though it had been celebrated hours beforehand. Another parishioner, whose parents' family had a wedding anniversary reception I attended, was discussing with her brothers how much they could drink. During this discussion she said, "Father Shane can hold his own," as if it was a badge of honor and I should be proud of this.

Then apparently, while at a Confirmation Mass at a nearby church with the Archbishop celebrating, I fell asleep during the service. Three boys said they saw me nodding off during the homily. I couldn't believe or accept this had transpired; I was embarrassed to think it could be true.

In 2009, signs were everywhere that my addiction was out of control, yet I refused to acknowledge I needed to seek outside support. One day, I asked my administrative assistant where one particular document was so I could sign it. She told me I had put my signature on the paper a week earlier. Was it a blackout? This frightened me. Soon thereafter, I woke up one Sunday morning to find the six-by-two-foot mirror behind my bedroom door had fallen and broke sometime during the night, with pieces scattered all over the floor as well as on the stairs. To this day, I still cannot comprehend how I came away from the breakage without causing a single wound on my body.

I went to the rectory from my office one early Thursday afternoon to take a nap since before lunch I was drinking and was now drowsy. About forty minutes into my snooze, my administrative assistant phoned notifying me that an unforeseen death of a parishioner had occurred, and his wife wished me to come to the home. Strangely, my staff member notified me that a policeman would drive me to and from the residence. I had not requested a ride. I guess she knew I was intoxicated and did not want me to drive.

Through these adverse episodes, I continued as a functional alcoholic and imagined my ministry at Saint Gregory was not impacted. After all, I attended faithfully to all the needs of the parish, was always on time for Mass and other meetings. I had very few blackouts. By all appearances, my life was in order, and I tried to fool myself into believing this.

Even in my foolishness, I really did believe my drinking had developed into an extremely grave situation. I actually did disclose my concerns to one parishioner, Lucy. One day, Lucy called me on the carpet. That December, she demanded that we meet over tea to discuss "a concern" she had about me. When I asked Lucy what the conversation was going to be about, she said that the purpose of our gathering could wait.

I suspected Lucy wished to talk over my drinking. Three days later, we made small talk before she questioned me if I knew what she wanted to speak with me about.

117

I replied, "My drinking."

Lucy answered, "Yes."

For the next ninety minutes, we discussed my alcohol cravings and what course of action I needed to take. Lucy said she would call the husband of a coworker who was involved with Alcohol Anonymous to inquire if he would give his name and phone number to me. The following day, she said that Jarrod would readily welcome a call from me. Before ending the conversation, she wanted me to promise her that I was going to contact Jarrod. I agreed to, although I was extremely nervous to follow through with this.

It was a Sunday afternoon when Lucy telephoned me. For over three hours, I tried to dial Jarrod's cell phone a minimum of ten times, only to end the call before it began to ring. My palms were sweating profusely as I sat at the top of the stairs for the duration of this time. Finally, I mustered enough courage to let the phone ring and then talked to Jarrod about my alcohol problem. Easygoing and supportive, he suggested that we meet the following day at a coffee shop in White Bear Lake.

On Monday afternoon, as we chatted at the coffee shop, he probed into the history of my addiction. As I told my story, he opened the "Big Book" of AA, asking me if I had heard about this book. I had. Jarrod asked me to read one chapter of the book aloud, which I did. We then had a discussion about what I had read. Upon concluding our conversation, he inquired if we could get together again the next week at the same locality. I accepted his suggestion and met with him the next Monday and the one thereafter. As we were just about to exit the coffee shop, Jarrod encouraged me to come to one of the AA meetings he attended on Sunday night, and offered to walk with me when going into the room. I replied, "Maybe, but I don't feel comfortable going." I said I would think about going to the meeting, knowing full well I had no intention of joining him on Sunday. After this meeting, I never saw Jarrod again.

I had another good friend, Denny, who questioned my drinking. He and his wife lived in Saint Paul, and they often allowed me to park my car in their driveway, and then they would take me to the airport whenever I would go on a trip. One time while driving me to the airport, he asked me why I had been drinking before coming to his house. He said he could always smell alcohol on my breath. He asked if I did not like flying. I replied that "at times I found flying sometimes boring." In a matter-of-fact voice, he reminded me of the seriousness of drinking and driving even if my blood alcohol was below the legal range.

I told him that I had just had one drink before arriving at his house. This was the truth. I would often carry a bottle of water which I would fill equally with vodka and water. I had stopped to drink it at a park a few miles before arriving at my friend's home. Then I would chew a mint or a piece of hard candy to try and mask my alcoholic breath. Of course, that never fooled my friend, a retired state trooper. While I was ashamed of my actions, I was grateful that he cared enough to voice his concern to me.

A permanent deacon was assigned to Saint Gregory the Great in the fall of 2008 and would minister at the parish until February 2012. He assisted me by preaching at Sunday Masses once a month and also assisted by visiting some of the sick within the parish. His wife also served our parish community by assisting couples prepare for the Sacrament of Matrimony.

Our deacon was also employed full-time at a large eastern suburban parish which was ninety miles round trip to North Branch. We regularly gathered for a meal to review his ministry and plan our schedules for the next few months. In order that he would not have to always drive to Saint Gregory's, I would often drive to meet him at a restaurant close to his work and meet over lunch. During these meetings, I was often nauseous and unable to eat due to my drinking the night before or because of my attempts to withdraw from alcohol. I lied to him by saying I wasn't hungry or was sick with a cold. During his entire ministry at the parish, he never commented on my alcohol dependence.

During this time, I would occasionally attempt to be honest with the people I consulted for support as I struggled to halt my alcohol addiction. I started seeing a new therapist in Saint Paul every other week. Additionally, I visited with a parishioner once or twice a month that I knew had been sober for several years.

I switched counselors hoping to get a grip and fresh view of my dependence from someone else. Through some Internet research, I decided on a male therapist, switching from a female whose specialty was addictions. My new therapist was Jewish. The fact he was a different faith than myself was unimportant to me. While he did have some basic knowledge of the Catholic faith and the priesthood, unlike my therapist before him (who was a Catholic), it did require that I regularly take the time to clarify myself in relation to being a Catholic priest during the therapy session.

Nonetheless, my therapist did help me improve my awareness of who I was and provided insight as to why I was drinking. Unfortunately, I did not always answer his questions honestly. I was honest in all areas of my life, but not about my drinking habits. One morning during one of our sessions, my therapist suspected I had been drinking before our meeting and asked me if I had. I denied it, but of course, I had.

After three years of counseling me, he informed me that he believed he could not be of further support. Reflecting back on this, I am convinced that he was well aware of my lying and manipulative behavior. This was an accurate assessment of my personality during this time of my life.

As I continued to confide in a parishioner about my addiction, I began to feel more comfortable and revealed with him the true particulars of my drinking. In a placid, nonjudging approach, the parishioner listened to me as I disclosed my story. He simply encouraged me to continue striving for sobriety each day. We visited regularly for over a year, then less frequently as time went on.

Amidst my drinking and pastoring my parish, the Archbishop and the Archdiocese of Saint Paul and Minneapolis called a meeting with all the priests of the diocese as they tried to come up with a strategy to deal with the declining church attendance among its over two hundred parishes. Priests gathered for consultations within their deaneries to discuss several models regarding the realignment of the parishes in their regions. Deaneries are geographical areas in a diocese. After bringing together all data from the deaneries, the leadership of the Archdiocese laid out their chart of action during the priests' conference.

It was decided that Saint Gregory the Great and Sacred Heart to the north, thirteen miles away from each other, were to be clustered in July 2012. When clustering two or more faith communities, each parish preserves its status as a stand-alone entity with separate pastoral and finance councils, individual assets, and particular Mass times. The change to the parishes was the sharing of a pastor and, in some circumstances, combining their staff.

In anticipation of the clustering of the two parishes, leadership representatives of both faith communities were invited to form a transitional committee joined by both pastors of each parish. This committee gathered for meetings to establish a strategy that would lead to a smooth transition when the time came for the actual coming together. Our meetings were usually productive, with each side presenting their understanding as to how they felt the parishes should proceed into the future and what hopes they had of me as their pastor.

Three months before the transition was to occur, the pastor of Sacred Heart became ill and soon went on a medical leave. The Archbishop appointed another priest as the temporary pastor until July 1st. However, for all practical purposes other than reaching final decisions on vital affairs, I was now responsible for spiritually and financially guiding Sacred Heart. I officially began my pastorate while sitting in an emergency room in Greensboro, North Carolina, with a dehydrated student while high school students from St. Gregory the Great Parish were on their annual mission trip. I joked with the teenager that I'd never expected to commence with my new responsibilities while in a hospital waiting room.

On the first weekend after our mission trip, I celebrated two Masses at Sacred Heart and then attended their welcoming reception for me. Providentially, two retired priests offered to assist me by helping to celebrate Mass at the two parishes twice a month. With this arrangement, I scheduled myself on alternate weekends at each parish. On Wednesdays, I would go to Sacred Heart for a morning Mass, followed by office hours. Although there was a townhouse-rectory in Rush City, I chose to continue living at the rectory in North Branch.

This transition to sharing a pastor between two churches created some uneasiness with the parishioners of the Sacred Heart faith community. They did not adjust well to having a nonresident pastor and believed that their needs would not be fulfilled. Although I spoke to them and tried assuring them I would be present as much as possible, they, nevertheless, believed I would spend the majority of my time at St. Gregory.

Unfortunately, I made the mistake of expecting the staff at Sacred Heart to operate their parish in the same manner as did the staff at Saint Gregory the Great. Naturally, this did not sit well with my northern parishioners.

Eight or nine months into my assignment, my treatment of the Sacred Heart parish community initiated a rift between the parishioners and myself. Therefore, I announced that a parish-wide meeting would be convened which would allow everyone to air their frustrations and apprehensions they might have concerning me and my pastoral approach. I stressed that the only unacceptable comments which would not be tolerated were destructive criticisms and character attacks on me or anyone else.

The number of parishioners who attended from Sacred Heart illustrated the care and love they had for their parish. The meeting progressed constructively, and I was pleased with the end results. Afterwards, I felt closer to the parishioners at Sacred Heart and believe I became a better shepherd to them. I started to see Sacred Heart as my second child, with its distinctive way of living out the Gospel, which I grew to love just as I had with my first child, or so to speak, Saint Gregory the Great.

By and large, the rest of the year at both parishes proceeded effortlessly. I felt content and comfortable in my new, more mature role as the pastor of two parishes in the northern half of Chisago County. Woefully, my alcohol addiction began affecting my ministry and health. Most of the time I felt physically miserable and struggled with thoughts of suicide. I continued to cycle between episodes of withdrawing for three days, drinking heavily for days, and then back again to withdrawing.

There were days that I could not eat at all. During the first day of withdrawing from alcohol, I literally thought of going to the hospital because I thought I would die. I would pack my backpack of clothes and toiletries and place it by the door in case I really had to go to the hospital.

On December 22, 2013, I stood in my living room when a thought came to me around 8:00 p.m. Standing for a long extent behind my sofa that divided the room creating two spaces, one to watch television and another a pseudo office area, I imagined what it would be like if I were away from the rectory for three months. How would I feel coming back after that time?

PART 3
2013–2019

*"To Know God is more
Important than to
Know About God"*

– Karl Rahner, S.J.

CHAPTER 18

The Attack

Heavy snow fell as Joan, a parishioner and friend, drove me in the middle of the night to Fairview Hospital in Wyoming, Minnesota, 19 miles away. The pain I was experiencing was excruciating and the hospital entrance couldn't come soon enough for me. As we pulled up, she entered the emergency waiting area to find a wheelchair, then hurried me inside and called out for assistance. Four hours later, I awoke, gazing upward while lying on a stretcher as a doctor looked down at me.

"We are not certain what is wrong with you. Also, we have no rooms available. Which hospital do you want us to transport you to?" questioned the doctor.

The first hospital that came to my mind was Cambridge Medical Center, part of Allina Health System which my own physician was part of.

"I guess Cambridge," I said weakly.

"We will have the ambulance take you over right away," responded the doctor.

The next thing I remembered, we were traveling slowly on Highway 95 in the middle of a ferocious snowstorm.

After being admitted to the hospital, I was brought up to a room on the fourth floor.[3] My condition worsened overnight as my organs began to fail and my blood pressure continued dropping. In the morning, since the medical staff still could not diagnose what

---

3   Many incidents in this chapter are recollections from my mom, Joan, and Doug.

was wrong with me, my doctor determined I should be transported to Abbott Northwestern Hospital, Minneapolis.

The winter storm was still in full force as I was transported by ambulance to Minneapolis. Joan rode in the ambulance with me and immediately upon our arrival, I was wheeled to the ICU unit.

I briefly regained consciousness when a doctor, a pancreas specialist, came into my room. He said my pancreas had grown to the size of a football. Joan inquired about my treatment options.

The doctor responded, "There are two choices. I can induce a medical coma to allow your pancreas, hopefully, to rest and heal. Or, you can ride it out, but most likely you will not recover and die. I will step out and return in thirty seconds for your answer as time cannot be wasted."

Even though I appeared cognizant since I was talking, I have no memory of this conversation. I looked at Joan and asked, "What should I do?"

She replied, "You need to have a medically induced coma so there is a chance you might live."

"Okay," I answered.

As the medical team worked quickly to induce my coma, Joan grabbed my hand and we started praying. We recited the "Our Father" and said our good-byes. This would be the last time I would be conscious for the next three weeks.

It was December 23rd, and over the next fifteen days, I lay in a coma as my pancreas began to heal. Joan contacted my mother, my close friend Doug, the parish offices, and others informing them of my acute pancreatitis attack. Doug came to the hospital right away. Since I had no family with me at this point, Joan remained at my side, unwilling to leave me alone. She was informed I was living minute by minute, without much hope of recovery.

The following day, I was told Father Tom Fitzgerald and Dan Graff came to see me. Father Fitz, my weekend assistant, anointed me with the Oil of the Sick. He then asked the doctor about my condition. The physician advised that at this point it was "touch and go."

For the remainder of the day as well as on Christmas, several parishioners, along with Doug and Joan, visited and prayed in the ICU room for me. Joan called and encouraged my mother to come right away since I was in a critical condition. My mother flew from Colorado and arrived at the hospital room on the afternoon of Christmas Day. She said she was overwhelmed and requested that everyone leave. The days following, she would only allow the few people she deemed important enough to visit me. I was told by many how hurtful it was to be turned away from visiting me. This was my mother's way of protecting me, even if this controlling behavior was not what I would have wanted.

I do not remember being taken off the respirator or coming out of the coma. I do hazily recall a male nurse at some point hanging pictures and cards from the children of my parishioners that offered their prayers and get-well wishes. I also somewhat remember this same nurse asking if I knew where I was, but then I drifted off to sleep again as I was still heavily medicated.

One day in mid-January, a week or two after coming out of my coma and having been transferred to another ICU room, I opened my eyes and stared at my surroundings. Off to the side, I saw someone. Once my eyes focused, I realized my mother was standing in the corner of the room and I shouted, "What are you doing here?" with a smile on my face. I was absolutely oblivious as to why I was in the hospital.

As Mom smiled back, she revealed, "You are a sick boy, and I am here to be with you."

Besides my mom's visits, several other friends came to see me, including my classmate Father Tim. He stopped by every week and took good care of Mom, bringing her to Mass and showing her how to get back and forth from Minneapolis to North Branch.

Joan dropped in from time to time bringing some small gifts. One present I loved was a framed picture of my nine-year-old cat named Jazira. I certainly wished that I could have held Jazira instead of just seeing a picture of her, but it was the next best thing. I was so glad Joan had brought Jazira to stay with my friend Agnes, as I knew she was comfortable, loved, and would be well cared for.

Once I was moved to recover in a standard hospital room, I not only began to comprehend the severity of the reason I was there, but also discovered I had temporarily lost the ability to write, walk, and talk. This created much anxiety and exasperation when I made an effort to use these skills. I struggled to communicate but could not speak with my trach tube still inside. I could not write, or even point to words or letters to spell out words. Having not used my leg muscles for so long, I had to regain strength and learn to walk again. Although I have no memory of doing this, my mother said when a newspaper was brought in, I would lick my finger to turn the pages as if I was reading it, which she found comical.

With the use of a walker, Mom walked alongside of me as we strolled the hospital corridors. One day a social worker inquired as to who was my power of attorney. I pointed out that I had no one. She asserted that I must select someone because of my health and then gave me a form to designate who that might be. I suggested choosing my friend Doug, who knew about and was handling my financial affairs since becoming ill.

Mom expressed her disagreement, specifying that it should be her since she was my next of kin.

"NO!" I said with authority.

Later, this "NO" became one of the most pinnacle decisions I ever made in my life. My stating "NO" so firmly changed me from being a "mama's boy" to becoming an adult man. This decision indisputably continues to transform me.

My mom made another choice for me when I was in the coma. During my stay at Abbott Northwestern, Mom along with Agnes and her daughter Margee and her husband Denny (the person who previously questioned my drinking when driving me to the airport) searched for a rehabilitation institution. After considering two other places around the Twin Cities, they determined that Bethesda Hospital, a place for long-term acute care for medically complex patients in Saint Paul, was the right one for my recovery.

Since I would be discharged soon, a doctor came in my room to remove my trach tube. He wrestled with it for the longest time; he could not get the trach to come out. As my mom agonizingly observed, I moaned from the intense pain he was causing with this struggle. He kept saying, "I have never had a problem taking out a trach," then continued his effort. Finally, after enduring so much agony in the procedure, he got it out. His difficulty of removing the trach has left a permanent scar, triggering frequent coughing spells, particularly when the air is dry.

On February 3rd, covered in blankets to keep me warm, I was transported by van, my wheelchair belted down, to Saint Paul. One of the staff members at Bethesda Hospital wheeled me to a fifth-floor room.

During my first few days at Bethesda, I was in such intense pain I felt like I was going to die. By the third day, most of the aches diminished with an increase of Oxycodone. Since I could not take anything by mouth, a feeding tube was used because all the medications needed to be crushed, put in water, and then shot through the PICC line on my left arm.

I begged my doctor to remove the feeding tube the first time she visited me at Bethesda. She stated possibly in a few days. Persistent in my request, after several days, the tube was disconnected, freeing me to eat, yet only on a liquid diet. It took several days to keep food down, which started one of several improvements to my health while residing at Bethesda.

The nurses and other staff were attentive to my requests as needed. Many of the personnel were gentle, caring, and friendly. I was able to get to know some of the employees fairly well seeing them day after day. At times, I would carry on casual conversations, primarily with the RNs, for they were in my room for longer periods.

During one conversation, an RN shared with me that early in her career, she feared giving shots to patients. To help her conquer this apprehension, the head nurse required her to give all the shots to patients for one full month, thus eliminating her fears entirely. Another RN, a gentleman from an Eastern African country, was rather tall and strong. Whenever the staff was repositioning me, he would lift me up, cradling me practically as one would a baby.

Now that I was stronger and awake for extended periods, visitors began to come to see me more frequently. Mom stayed with me every day through mid-February. When she felt that I was on my way to a full recovery, she flew back to Colorado in the middle of February. Numerous parishioners sent get-well cards or came to visit. Three of those visits particularly remain in my memory.

A former grounds caretaker at Saint Gregory the Great, Zack, a college student, dropped by one day to say hello and requested a letter of recommendation for an internship he was applying to for the summer. I was incapable of typing this out myself, so writing the reference took a considerable amount of exertion and required me to keep sending it back and forth to my administrative assistant before I was finally content with the recommendation.

Another parishioner stopped by one afternoon after getting off from her work that was close by. As we discussed my acute pancreatitis attack, she probed into what had caused it to happen. Until that moment, I never honestly and directly disclosed the reason for my illness to anyone who was not aware of the circumstances.

"Because of my drinking of alcohol," I revealed to her.

The parishioner responded by uttering, "Oh." She did not give the impression that she was shocked by this revelation.

The first week of the Minnesota weather in 2014 was taxing at times with heavy snowfall and frigid temperatures. One snowy day, a friend came from North Branch for a chat. My initial meeting with Richard happened when we were at home with a mutual acquaintance a few years previously. Over the years, I continued to patronize his business and get better acquainted with him. The prior summer, we drove to Forest Lake where I apprehensively attended my first AA Twelve Step meeting. We went together three or four times, and not once did I talk during the meetings. Later in early fall, I would attend a meeting alone and talk briefly.

My relationship with Richard at the time was limited to doing business with him and gathering at the rectory to discuss my addiction. Consequently, I was surprised to see him when he walked in to visit me. Since he was not positive that I had an AA Big Book with me, he carried one wrapped in newspaper, which he handed to me. I was appreciative for his thoughtfulness. As he sat on a ledge next to my bed, we talked about my illness and alcoholism for over an hour.

When there were no visitors, I either slept or listened to background music from the television. Four or five days a week, I was wheeled down to physical therapy. Disliking this activity, I grumbled relentlessly more days than not. Nonetheless, the staff demonstrated patience and understanding while continually pushing me along in my recovery.

I walked through the halls with a walker with a staff member at my side in case of a fall. As I became stronger, these strolls grew more frequent and longer. I particularly relished pausing at one end of the hallway where I could view the Minnesota State Capitol, which was two blocks away, and the Cathedral of Saint Paul a little farther down Archbishop John Ireland Boulevard. After three weeks, the staff allowed family and friends to join me in my walks and permitted additional journeys down the hallways.

On one occasion, my doctor spoke to me about my alcoholism and the importance of never drinking again. She specified that if I ingested even one drink, it could have serious consequences, including the possibility of death. I believe that she was striving to make a compelling case for me not to take any chances with my health.

On March 1, I was released from Bethesda Hospital and entered a rehabilitation center in Anoka, Minnesota. At this time, I no longer required medical treatment and further intensified physical therapy was prescribed for my recovery. I had a private room with a view of the railroad tracks, allowing me to see and hear the trains traveling past with regularity—something I thoroughly enjoyed.

During my stay in Anoka, I learned to shower by myself again after having cautiously protected the drainage tube on my left side. Also, with the support of a walker, I was able to stroll around the building and to the dining room. I was eating regularly but on a restricted diet. With every passing day, I became sturdier in my activities and more and more independent.

Every day, a staff member would take me to physical or mental health therapy. The staff usually received my cooperation for physical strengthening. On the other hand, I was stubborn and resistant to many tasks I had to do regarding my mental health evaluations.

In one incident, my therapist requested that I call a local hardware store and ask if they had a specific brand of paint. At first, I refused. However, she stipulated that I could not leave that day's session until making the telephone call. Another time she told me I had to learn how to make toast. I angrily replied back, "I know how to do that!"; however, I still was forced to accomplish this task. By the end of the third week, the staff assessed that I was well enough to return to North Branch.

The premonition I had the night before initially becoming ill and heading off to the emergency room had turned into a reality. I had now been absent from my duties for three and a half months.

CHAPTER 19

Cheating Death

For the next two months, I couldn't handle the stairs, so I lived in the living room and slept on the navy-blue leather sofa night and day. Conveniently the kitchen was around the corner. Unable to speedily get up to answer the door, a sign was posted on it notifying guests to come in during the day and early evening hours.

Each day, I ordinarily welcomed a few guests who were predominantly parishioners. One of my parishioners, Claire, a good friend and RN, would stop over to check on me, caring for me and making sure I stayed on track. Moreover, I received home health care from a registered nurse for about two months. During this time, I was mainly alone for extended periods, thankful for having the television as company. Operating a vehicle for the time being was still out of the question.

The Archbishop allowed me to remain on a medical leave through the fall so that my body could fully mend itself. This permitted me to feel less guilty for lying around all day. Despite that, I eagerly desired to resume working, return to my office, and celebrate Mass. Most days, I was jaded with little ability to do anything. A month upon coming home, on Easter Sunday morning, I concelebrated Mass with Father Fitzgerald. Then, another month later, I began celebrating Mass once every Sunday.

Numerous doctor appointments were scheduled during this period. Due to the fact I could not drive myself, a handful of parishioners volunteered to bring me to the hospital or clinics. Because of my ascites, there were two hospital visits in order that the fluid could be removed from my abdomen—a lengthy and boring procedure. During one of these appointments, I saw the pancreas specialty doctor who had diagnosed my acute pancreatitis when at Abbott Northwestern. He revealed to me how unbelievably blessed I was to be alive. He denoted honestly that it was a miracle that I had come through my life-threatening ordeal. I had defeated all likelihood of death!

At the time for fear of dying, as one would expect, I no longer drank any alcoholic beverages except for wine at Holy Eucharist, which Catholics believe becomes the real blood of Christ. There was no yearning to consume the spirits that nearly killed me. I finally wanted to indefinitely avoid alcohol.

In relation to lifelong sobriety, I scheduled a meeting with a chemical dependency counselor for the latter part of April. On the day of the appointment, for the first time since ending up in the hospital, I drove myself fourteen miles to Cambridge. To begin with, I was given a chemical dependency assessment followed up with her recommendations. The suggestions were to some extent similar to ones I'd received eight years ago when I was in the psychiatric unit overnight.

First, the counselor sternly encouraged me to return to AA meetings. I responded by saying, "Maybe." Then I questioned whether she knew of any good therapists in the area whose specialty was in the field of addictions. She said matter-of-factly, "Yes, there is a superb one in Isanti," the next town south of Cambridge. She presented a business card with the therapist's contact information. Before departing, she once again recommended that I soon attend AA, reminding me that I could not remain sober without the support of others.

She was right! At the end of May, I purchased a bottle of wine, consuming it in two days, disregarding precious advice from doctors. I anticipated there would be some repercussions, but none came to pass. I comprehended drinking heavily was not a possibility, but I still believed I could drink once more without dying from it. Throughout June, I guardedly kept on drinking. I never drank more than a bottle of wine, and I avoided hard liquor.

Unsurprisingly, I lied to everyone about my return to alcohol usage, which led to guilt. Whenever someone asked why I drank, whether Mom, a friend, or colleague, I began to present my motives. The answers I offered were because I'd just experienced a magnificent day, or I had a lonely and boring day, or the fact that I was distressed about something. Looking back, I guess that that would excuse just about everything!

Often after undergoing a successful morning or evening, I came back to the rectory desiring to celebrate it. With nobody around, I turned to alcohol, as it would give to me an opportunity to feel even happier about the earlier positive results of the day. Other days, I simply was depressed, needing a boost in my emotional state. Once two or three drinks were gulped down, I would no longer feel isolated or disenchanted—not surprisingly until the subsequent morning.

Sporadically, having either a bad day or being worried about something, I would use alcohol to lift up my mood. Negative incidents or circumstances were other reasons that led to my drinking from time to time. However, I always thought that awful days rarely provoked me to drown my feelings away, at least not as much as when I had a positive day.

As time went on, I asked myself: how and why could I engage in this pattern again, when merely six months prior it practically laid me into the grave? Something had to be done.

At long last, I finally arranged for an appointment with the counselor in Isanti. The subsequent week in July, I met with my new therapist Gracelyn. After fifteen minutes with her, I knew instantaneously that I had found my new therapist. Not only could I relate to her effortlessly, but also by chance, she was Catholic. Contrasting to my former shrink, our conversations lacked any need to expound on the workings of the Catholic Church or the role of priests. This was appreciated since it allotted more time to get to my purpose of meeting with her and the heart of why I continued to drink alcohol.

In the beginning I saw Gracelyn weekly, then every two weeks, followed by monthly for the next three years. For a while, I lied to her about how much or how often I was consuming alcoholic beverages. Gracelyn listened to me and gently challenged me, waiting patiently until the day I would be truthful. Like a turtle, I was extremely slow in moving to the stage where I became utterly honest.

The moment I started to be absolutely honest with Gracelyn, was the moment I began to figure out myself why I drank, thus creating longer intervals between my days of drinking. Additionally, since meeting with her, I was showing up at weekly AA meetings in Forest Lake. In the early days, I persisted in being quiet, barely disclosing anything about myself at the meetings. As months passed, and I became comfortable and accustomed with the group, I shared more and socialized briefly after the meetings.

I made strides and drank less wine and liquor and sought support in attempts to become sober, but by September, it was too late to prevent me from developing another disease. I drove to see my primary doctor for my yearly physical. Leaving her office, I presumed that my health was as good as it could be considering what I went through that recent year.

On my way back to North Branch during rush hour, my cell phone rang. Noticing that the caller ID was the Allina Health Isles Clinic, I answered the phone, saying, "Hello, this is Shane."

"Hi Shane, this is Dr. McMillan, can you come back to the clinic today?" she asked.

"Why?" I responded.

"Your A1C is high—way too high. You are now a diabetic and really need to return today and get started with an insulin regimen."

Responding that I could not, since I wanted to avoid rush hour and get home, she then inquired, "Can you come back tomorrow?"

"I can," I informed Dr. McMillan, then went on to ask what time I was to return.

She informed me that I would be seeing her nurse assistant at noon. Thus, I traveled back down to Minneapolis the following day to initiate a lifelong treatment of insulin shots.

During the year 2015, I began to feel frustrated that I could not end my addiction. Hence, I invited Richard to drop in for a visit at the rectory and sought out his advice. I mentioned my relentless struggles and desire to be sober.

"I know alcohol is a poison. I want to quit, but I cannot. Will I ever be capable of stopping? I do not believe I will ever quit," I lamented.

"One day it will just click, and you will stop," Richard confidently responded.

"It will," I answered back, not swayed by his remark.

Richard uttered, "Yes, it will click, just be patient."

His conviction that one day I would stop stayed with me. Our conversation lingered in the back of my mind.

I encountered extended periods of abstinence from alcohol and spent fewer days drinking alcoholic beverages. Along with therapy and AA meetings, my thoughts and feelings became clearer in my head, which then allowed me to develop further emotionally and grow deeper spiritually. Without pouring poison into my body and exchanging the spirits of alcohol for the Spirit of God, I began to fathom the effects of my birth father's tragic death, as well as growing up in a family environment that allowed for little to no expression of one's valid feelings. These twofold dynamics in turn created a sense of abandonment and the fear of expressing my feelings and needs, both of which led me to escape through the use of alcohol. Moreover, with my competency in handling financial affairs throughout most of my life, I usually had money to purchase material possessions wastefully; that was another means to mask my overwhelming negative feelings.

As time elapsed and my brain was no longer foggy, I discovered just how much I despised life and myself. I did not savor living one speck! In fact, astonishingly, I pondered why I'd never followed through with any of my suicide attempts over the years while drinking? The lone factor, I believed, for not taking my life was my faith in God. As appalling as living was for me, there always was a smidgeon of hope.

Yet, even more amazingly was learning that while I was dependent on alcohol, to a large extent, I had not been keen in my life as a Catholic priest. Even though by all outward appearances I appeared to be happy, in reality, I learned that this was not the situation in my clear head. Twenty-plus years had passed since my ordination as a priest, yet, I kept on feeling insecure preaching at Mass or other prayer services. Moreover, lingering doubts about my self-worth persisted. I knew others had a hard time understanding me as my speech impediment and dyslexic thoughts often caused them to ask me to repeat myself, again feeling totally inadequate socially.

There was evidence that my feelings of worthlessness were valid both personally and in the Archdiocese. Family and friends seldom called. I wished to be of service outside of my parishes in the larger local church community. Thus, I had offered to be a member of some Archdiocesan committees and sought to be a supervisor in a seminary program; however, invitations to join were at no time forthcoming, thus leaving me feeling isolated and insignificant.

During my drinking days, alcohol served as my only "friend," who would always be faithful and present for me when I needed a distraction or comfort from my mostly unpleasant life, as one would expect. My hopeless existence would become bearable the minute I swallowed liquor. Under the manipulative powers of alcohol in my body, I felt fearless, confident, worthy, and content—or thus I accepted as truth. Most of the time, I definitely was not concerned about what the alcohol was doing, the "good friend" it was for me. A never-ending dislike of myself as well as aversion to living my life endured.

Two years after coming out of my coma, a transformation was taking place in how I viewed myself and in life. Besides being in therapy with Gracelyn and going to AA meetings, two relationships, a pilgrimage, and an article would create a turning point in my alcoholism.

For the first time as an adult, I now felt absolutely accepted and loved for who I was by my counselor as well as a few other individuals. Even with my brokenness, imperfections, and past, they accepted me for me, without any judgement. At the moment of feeling completely accepted, the process of starting to love myself, life, and God emerged anew! I now valued my life, appreciated life, and worshiped the one true God. At last, I believed that I knew God and not just knew about God.

My worldview transformed immensely. Now, I saw God, Sacred Scripture, life and people, all in a new light. Coming away from my near-death encounter imparted me with a sense of a second chance at life. The rebirth I underwent powerfully prompted almost everything I felt and thought with new perceptions and a new way of seeing my world.

Interpreting Bible passages came with new insights. Such as Jesus' commandment found in Mark 12:31, "The second (commandment) is this, 'You shall love your neighbor as yourself.'" Now, I understood the importance of loving yourself first. If you cannot love yourself, you undoubtedly cannot love your neighbor, as we are called to do by Jesus. Since I began to love myself, I started having greater love for others.

Another example is in April 2016, when my friend Fr. Neil from the US Virgin Islands, and I traveled on a pilgrimage to Europe. On the itinerary were places I wished to visit such as Fatima in Portugal, the location of a Blessed Virgin Mary's apparition; Avila, Spain, the home of the Carmelite Saint Teresa; and Lisieux, France, the Shrine of Saint Thérèse. Likewise, on the schedule, the two locations I absolutely wanted to explore were Loyola, Spain, home of Saint Ignatius of Loyola, and Cluny, France, the spot and remnants of the once largest and most powerful Benedictine Abbey in Western Civilization. The one site I had no desire to stop at was Lourdes, France, another site apparition of the Blessed Virgin Mary; however, every pilgrimage we looked at included Lourdes. To make matters even less attractive, it was the longest stay we would have at any locale—three days.

When we completed our journey, I had been disappointed with my trip to Cluny Abbey, for it had been anticlimactic after thirty years of yearning to go there. On the other hand, the Lourdes visit was the most spiritual. At Lourdes, as in the stopover in Loyola where I concelebrated Mass at the chapel where Saint Ignatius had his spiritual conversion, I felt closest to God. I never ever expected to encounter my time in Lourdes as a highlight of my European pilgrimage.

Sometime later in 2016, my counselor Gracelyn gave me an article called "I Am Your Disease."[4] When I left her office that day, I read

---

4   See Appendix.

and reread this influential article. I consider this one commentary on the disease of alcohol as one of the foremost roots for the transformation that was about to materialize in me.

On a Friday night in November 2016, Richard's assertion the previous year that "someday it will just click" appeared. That night I consumed my last alcoholic beverage.

CHAPTER 20

~~

A Second Life

The longer I stayed away from alcohol, the more I felt as if I were living for the very first time, seeing the world with new eyes, and feeling energized to live life. During 2017 and during my sabbatical, I realized I had come to accept myself as I was. I started feeling more self-confident, and many of my fears started to disappear. These attributes became evident during three various occasions.

In March, Brother Bede from the Brother Emmanuel's Camaldolese religious community in Big Sur called to let me know of my uncle's death on March 6. Two weeks earlier at the age of eighty-nine, he fell and broke his hip, and quickly became seriously ill and passed away. Brother Bede indicated that the date and time of my uncle's funeral Mass was to be determined later due to the recent heavy rains in California that washed out much of Highway 1, which led to the religious community entrance.

A few days later, the hermitage's superior, Prior Father Cyprian, notified me by e-mail that the funeral service was arranged for March 17. He wrote asking if I would attend, and I replied back saying I would get back to him in a day or two. A day later, I e-mailed to say I would indeed be attending the funeral. I flew out a few days later and was the only family member present.

As the main highway in front of the Camaldoli Hermitage to the north was closed, I was advised to follow the hearse the morning of the funeral onto the back roads from King City. When we arrived at the gates of the hermitage, Father Cyprian and his community greeted us. Immediately, Uncle Emmanuel's coffin was carried to the church where it remained open until the service an hour later.

Father Cyprian invited me to assist him during the Mass by reciting some of the prayers. Following the service, a procession proceeded out of the church around the corner to the small community cemetery. When the brief burial prayers concluded, as my uncle's body was lowered, I thought about this holy man who had lived at the hermitage for over fifty years and had led a contemplative, humble life faithfully serving his community and God. This world was enough for him to be happy and feel peaceful because he lived for God alone, completely indifferent to what others might have thought of him.

Even though my own life may seem insignificant in the eyes of the world, it is significant in the eyes of God. Others can judge me, yet there is only one judge and that is God. Some people have already made up their minds on how a priest should act, talk, behave, and even look. Charismatic priests will get the larger parishes, parishioners will invite them out to their homes for meals, and they will be asked to serve on various committees within a diocese. I am a priest who is an introvert, difficult to understand due to a speech impediment. None of that matters. The truth of who I am is that I am a beloved child of God my Creator. I am a gift from God. God loves me and I now love myself! These insights have made me the happiest I have ever been in adulthood, minus the alcohol.

Our parish youth participate in the annual summer mission trip through an organization founded by some friends, Jim and Heather, titled "Alive in You": Catholic Conference and Service Camps. Every year since 2010, with the exception of one year, I have participated in the six-day AiY program to accompany our students and chaperones on worksites, as well as provide priestly ministry as needed.

I remember when we traveled to Greensboro in 2012. The AiY liturgist called me several times to see if I would celebrate one or two daily Masses and hear confessions on a Friday night. I said I would get back to her after checking my schedule. During our initial conversation and the ones that followed, I knew that I could help. Truthfully, I felt insecure about being in front of four hundred students and their chaperones, and unenthusiastic about hearing confessions. Despite these feelings, I did accept the invitation to assist during the week and managed to celebrate a Mass and hear confessions, apprehensive as I was.

Five years later in 2017, we drove to St. Louis for our yearly mission trip. After arriving, before the new AiY liturgist had an opportunity to ask for assistance with the sacramental needs of the week, I willingly extended my priestly ministry. I agreed to celebrate Mass, beginning with the opening service that would be held outside on the lawn. All through the week, I self-confidently offered my services without reluctance.

During the opening weeks of my five-and-a-half-month sabbatical, in October 2018, I flew unaccompanied to Edinburgh, Scotland. I took a tram to the train station, a train ride to Perth, and then a taxi to the Redemptorists Saint Mary's Monastery on Kinnoull Hill for a seven-week spiritual and renewal course. This was the first time away from Minnesota for an extended period during my sobriety.

After having worked on conquering my fear of others, when our group of 16 and three facilitators gathered for introductions, I was slightly anxious to reveal any information about myself. Nevertheless, one of my goals during this sabbatical was to become more outgoing and comfortable with myself. I quickly learned that I was in the remarkable company of several priests, religious sisters, and a laywoman who allowed me to be myself. I felt relaxed and at ease enough to disclose personal information—something I never thought I would be able to do.

I sought to defeat my fear of people through honesty and openness. No longer fogged by the effects of alcohol, to my surprise, I felt little anxiety observing events going on around me. I was also learning that I was capable of revealing myself and could seek what I needed and ask questions that I could never ask before. I could eat breakfast fast and leave, like one of the religious sisters, and not feel guilty. During a Friday morning small group session, I shared my thoughts more quickly instead of always being the last one to interject. In this group, for the first time ever, I revealed I was an alcoholic.

Our speakers lectured on interesting topics, even if some of the material wasn't new to me. I interacted with my entire group, switching seats sometimes in order to visit with all fifteen persons in our sabbatical community. While in session, there was always a question and answer time. While previously I would just listen, this time I actually raised my hand, asking for clarification on this or that.

Since we had free time from Friday afternoon to Sunday evening, I spent this time traveling with others or even sometimes alone. I flew to Dublin one weekend, rode the train to Aberdeen, stayed at a hotel, and toured Edinburgh alone.

One Sunday afternoon, Father Paul from Australia and I climbed 246 steps to the top of William Wallace's monument in Sterling. When we reached the bottom of the monument after going up, I bravely disclosed that I was afraid of heights—something I would have never revealed before. On another trip to Glasgow, I had no qualms telling what I did or did not like. I observed Paul's fearlessness in speaking with strangers or employees at a place we were patronizing, learning from him to be unafraid, to interact and ask questions.

During the interim between Scotland and Cocoa Beach, Florida, I flew back to Minnesota to visit my gravely ill friend Agnes. We talked. When her son Tom left the room to retrieve something, Agnes asked me if dying was like going to sleep. I replied, "Yes, a peaceful sleep." After an hour-long visit, we said our good-byes and told each other of our love for one another. Agnes died a week later. Instead of drowning my sadness with alcohol, I allowed myself to feel the grief.

In Cocoa Beach, I began to work on my physical self as well. Working out every day and eating healthy was a goal of mine. I even had a personal trainer, Derek, whose encouragement kept me motivated. I was present most mornings for daily Mass at Our Savior Catholic Church. Before my illness, I would not have gone that often, if at all. I also went on numerous walks and had dinner regularly with the pastor, Father Val, sharing honestly on many topics including personal ones—something I would have never done before my transformation. This pastor became my friend. The main road through Cocoa Beach, Highway A1A, was busy with heavy traffic. When getting onto, off, or while stopped at a stoplight, my patience actually increased. When I was drinking, I was very impatient. Now, without the effects of alcohol in my body, my fears, specifically of people, disappeared. As silly as it sounds, I used to fear calling to order a pizza. I once believed that alcohol helped me to be brave, yet that was a lie. Now I live life fearlessly.

As I looked out at the waves of the vast Atlantic Ocean each day, not once did I tire of God's creation in front of me. I have joy for life!

I used to believe that alcohol was my "best friend." How crazy and insane was that thinking! Alcohol, which I had placed my confidence in, only gave me a false sense of courage and confidence. I had been as slow as a turtle crossing the road to come to the realization that only the Spirit of God can make me fearless, self-confident, truly happy, and give me the desire to live life to the fullest.

CHAPTER 21

Conclusion

The one consistent theme prevailing throughout my life has been God's presence. I have always believed in God, but my ability to encounter God, the one true living God, the God of Abraham, the God of Isaac, and the God of Jacob, was obscured by my addiction to alcohol.

Like coastal fog that can sometimes shroud the magnificence of the Atlantic Ocean, so too has alcohol hindered me from seeing and feeling the splendor of God. Not until the haze of alcohol was entirely eliminated from my body could I know the one true God whose presence is felt through the third person of the Holy Trinity—the Holy Spirit. My new empowering awareness of God has allowed me totally to turn over my life to Him. This new understanding of God has allowed me to begin tackling my alcohol dependency directly. I continued to grow in my conversion as I became more grateful for the many blessings God has conferred on me.

One of the marks of a true disciple of Jesus Christ is when he or she displays signs of gratitude daily. My treasured friend Agnes, in all the years I knew her, was grateful for everything: her blessings, her family, her friends, and most of all her faith. For that reason, she was happy and joyful. Agnes taught me how to be grateful! Moreover, having an attitude of thankfulness keeps me on the path of sobriety. Whenever I might be struggling to persevere in my sobriety or feel depressed, I remember to give myself an extra dose of gratitude, and this can carry me through any troubled time that may arise.

My heart has a sense of appreciativeness for living in this time and place. Had I been born fifty years earlier, I probably would not have been permitted to be a priest due to my inability to learn Latin. Had I not lived near Abbott Northwestern Hospital, one of the most distinguished and technically advanced hospitals in the United States, I would not have survived my illness. Had I not discovered unconditional acceptance without judgement by my last therapist and a friend, I would not have learned to love myself enough to stop drinking myself to death.

Choosing to surrender to God, endeavoring to embrace a spirit of poverty, and serving others are graces which have given me hope and joy. The words of Jesus in the Gospels and the lessons I learned in AA have taught me that letting God be in charge of your life and accepting whatever may happen to you without resistance is crucial. Jesus surrendered his human existence to his Father above in his crucifixion. The third step in AA states, "Made a decision to turn our will and our lives over to the care of God as we understand Him." The moment I surrendered myself completely to God, I no longer desired to drink. Having allowed God to be in the driver's seat, and living His plan for me, produced an abundance of tranquility in my life.

From the Beatitudes in the Gospel of Matthew, Jesus proclaimed that "Blessed are the poor in spirit, for theirs is the kingdom of heaven" (Mt 5:3). An attitude of "poor in spirit" goes a long way. When I have fewer material possessions, live life simply and fast, my yearning for alcohol is converted into a yearning for God. While on sabbatical in Scotland and Cocoa Beach, I carried with me only a few items of clothing and personal belongings. Having minimal items in each of my rooms, fewer choices exist. Fewer choices and distractions allow me more time to listen to God and surrender myself to his will, which lessens my desire to take a drink.

The third practice I need to exercise is a life of service. The ideas of Jesus and the practices of AA emphasize doing for others, which brings me out of myself. I identify service loosely. Service can be accomplished through the traditional manner of recognizing it in such ways as working at a soup kitchen or painting a house while on a mission trip. Saying words of kindness to a store clerk who appears to be having a bad day or offering up my seat on a bus to an elderly person are actions of service that bring me out of myself and force me to focus on another. Sponsoring someone in AA is another form of service. Carrying out service in my daily interactions is a weapon in my arsenal which helps keep me sober.

I have been so blessed throughout my life. Out of my birth Dad and Mom's love for each other, I received the gift of life. I was not appreciative of this gift for many years during my alcoholism, but then God allowed me to encounter a near-death experience with an acute pancreatitis attack to once again appreciate my life. God has blessed me with a second chance to live. Amidst my suffering, with my faith in God, I was capable of seeing his goodness and love through it all.

I have learned to take care of this gift of life at a turtle's pace. Like a turtle, I have crossed the road, going from the love of alcohol across to the other side to the love of God—a side where self-confidence, freedom, and fearlessness have been found, allowing me a life of hope, and joy.

Appendix

I AM YOUR DISEASE

You know who I am, you've called me your friend
Wishes of misery and heartache I send
I want only to see that you're brought to your knees
I'm the devil inside you, I am your disease.
I'll invade all your thoughts, I'll take hostage your soul
I'll become your new master, in total control
I'll maim your emotions, I'll run the whole game
Till your entire existence is crippled with shame
When you call me, I come, sometimes in disguise
Quite often I'll take you by total surprise
But take you I will, and just as you've feared
I'll want only to hurt you, with no mercy spared
If you have your own family, I'll see it's destroyed
I'll steal every pleasure in life you've enjoyed
I'll not only hurt you, I'll kill if I please
I'm your worst living nightmare, I am your disease
I bring self-destruction, but still you can't tell
I'll sweep you through heaven, then drop you in hell
I'll chase you forever, wherever you go
And then when I catch you, you won't even know
I'll sometimes lay silent, just waiting to strike
What's yours becomes mine, cuz I take what I like
I'll take all you own, and I won't care who sees
I'm your constant companion... I am your disease
If you have any honor, I'll strip it away

THE TURTLE PRIEST

You'll lose all your hope and forget how to pray
I'll leave you in darkness, while blindly you stare
I'll reduce you to nothing, and won't even care
So, don't take for granted my powers sublime
I'll bend, and I'll break you, time after time
I'll crumble your world with the greatest of ease
I'm that madman inside you...I am your disease
But today I'm real angry...you want to know why?
I let this treatment center full of Addicts entirely slip by
How did I lose you? Where did I go wrong?
One minute I had you...then next you were gone
You just can't dismiss all the good times we've shared
When you were alone...wasn't it I who appeared?
When you sold those possessions you knew you would need
Wasn't I the first one who stepped in and agreed
Now look at you bastards, you're all thinking clear
You escaped with your lives when you found your way here
Only fools think they're winners when admitting defeat
It's what you must say when you're claiming that seat
Go ahead and surrender, if that's what you choose
But, I'm not giving up, cuz I can't stand to lose
So stand in your groups and support hand in hand
Better choices will save you...leaving me to be damned
Well, be damned all you people seeking treatment each week
Be damned inner strength, however unique
Be damned all your sayings, be damned your clichés
Be damned every addict, who back to me strays
For I know it will happen, I've seen it before
Those who love misery will crawl back for more
So take comfort in knowing, I'm waiting right here
But next time around, you'd just better beware
You think that you're stronger or smarter this time

APPENDIX

There isn't a mountain or hill you can't climb
Well if that's what you're thinkin', you ain't learned a thing
I'll still knock you silly if you step back in my ring
But you say you've surrendered, so what can I do?
It's so sad in a way, I had big plans for you
Creating your nightmare for me was a dream
I'm sure gonna miss you...we made quite a team
So please don't forget me, I won't forget you
I'll stand by your side watching all that you do
I'm ready and waiting, so call if you please
I won't let you forget me...I am your disease

Author Unknown

CPSIA information can be obtained
at www.ICGtesting.com
Printed in the USA
BVHW081306110921
616352BV00004B/19

9 781977 221346